BAKING IMPERFECT

Thunder Bay Press
An imprint of Printers Row Publishing Group
9717 Pacific Heights Blvd, San Diego, CA 92121
www.thunderbaybooks.com • mail@thunderbaybooks.com

Thunder Bay Press
Publisher: Peter Norton
Associate Publisher: Ana Parker
Editor: Traci Douglas

Hamlyn, Octopus Group
Publishing Director: Eleanor Maxfield
Art Director: Yasia Williams
Senior Editor: Pollyanna Poulter
Production Manager: Caroline Alberti
Illustrations: Hiller Goodspeed
Photography: Tom Regester
Home Economist: Henrietta Clancy
Prop Stylist: Agathe Gits

Library of Congress Control Number: 2022936453

ISBN: 978-1-6672-0201-3

Printed in China

26 25 24 23 22 1 2 3 4 5
The Great British Bake Off Baker logo™ is licensed by Love Productions Ltd.

BAKING IMPERFECT

CRUSH, WHIP, AND SPREAD IT LIKE NOBODY'S WATCHING

LOTTIE BEDLOW

THUNDER BAY
P·R·E·S·S

San Diego, California

Contents

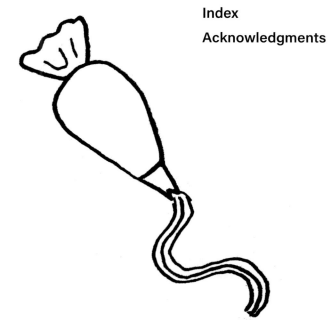

Introduction

DOES ANYONE EVEN READ RECIPE BOOK INTRODUCTIONS?

I know I don't. But I have been asked to write one, so…

My name is Lottie and I taught myself to bake through trial and error. Bored and scrolling on the loo one day, I decided to apply for a place in a TV baking competition (for which I was wholly underqualified and underprepared). And in a bizarre turn of events, I got in. My entire life is now all about baking and trying to encourage nervous bakers to have a go too.

The world of baking is daunting, there is no doubt about it. To an outsider it can feel like a secretive, elitist, sticky little cult. I know because I used to be an outsider. Using Instagram for inspiration, I would be left feeling like a talentless, clumsy failure, who also just happened to be the world's worst food photographer. That's because Instagram rarely shows you the mistakes. But we're all making them, all the time. So I vowed to be honest when it came to my baking—to celebrate the little mishaps and the epic disasters, to share my trials, errors, and successes with you. And in doing this, I hope to convince even the most unlikely, inexperienced, and apprehensive bakers to get stuck in. Because, really, what's the worst that could happen?

WHAT KIND OF RECIPES ARE IN THE BOOK?

Most of the chapter titles are fairly self-explanatory—Risk It for a **Biscuit**, **Cakes** are Boring, You're **Bready** for This, Don't Be Scared of **Pastry**, and Give Me **Puddings**, Not Hugs—up until the final chapter, Pass It On, Please, which features an assortment of ideas inspired by family and friends. There's a mix of sweet and savory, and it's worth pointing out that the pastry chapter includes basic instructions for making your own shortcrust (savory and sweet), hot water crust, choux, and (semi) rough puff pastry, which feature in the main recipes. Essentially, I've aimed to bring together a collection of recipes that just taste really, really good.

HOW HARD ARE THE RECIPES?

I've developed a highly sophisticated cracked egg system to give you a sense of how much of a challenge each recipe might be. The number of cracked eggs above each recipe's hilarious title tells you how hard I think it is. One cracked egg means you can do this recipe even if you have no idea what baking means. Five cracked eggs means I struggled and think it's difficult but worth it. If you know how scales of 1 to 5 work, I'm sure you get the rest. And even though there are recipes of varying difficulty within each chapter, as a rule, cookies are the easiest and normally the best place to start for a newbie.

WHAT IF THINGS GO WRONG?

Which they will. So almost all of the recipes include hints, tips, or troubleshooting guidance for if and when things go south. These are real fixes for incidents that happened to me when writing the recipe, so I know they work. Sometimes you might have to just start again. Sad.

LASTLY…

I just want to say thank you for buying this book, or at least reading the intro while standing in a discount book store. I never thought I'd be able to write a book, let alone a recipe book, and it is all of you who have made it possible. If I can bake, anyone can, and that includes you. So, give it a go. And when things go a bit wrong, just remember, **who cares as long as it tastes good?**

WHAT DO I NEED TO KNOW BEFORE GETTING STARTED?

1) Before starting each recipe, please READ THE WHOLE THING first so that you have some idea of what's involved before you jump in. You don't want to begin making a dessert when your dinner party guests are half an hour away only to come across a "let soak overnight" situation.

2) And that reminds me: I've not included estimated preparation or oven times because I don't want you to rush or feel like you're doing a bad job if it takes you double, triple, or even quadruple the amount of time I said it would. Look at the bake time and the steps involved in the prep, and give yourself the time you need to enjoy the process.

3) I've also omitted specifying how much a recipe makes or how many it serves. I would rather not be that prescriptive and instead give you scope to make individual bakes or portions a bit larger or smaller, depending on what kit you have or your personal preference (appetite).

4) Each recipe has a Kit List, but I haven't included the more everyday kitchen items. I have assumed, perhaps incorrectly, that you will have access to an oven, regular cutlery and tools, bowls, saucepans, roasting pan, sieve, rolling pin, cutting board, and some kind of wire rack for cooling etc., along with a stock of plastic wrap, foil, and parchment paper for lining cookie sheets and pans. You'll also need some decent kitchen scales, a set of measuring spoons, and a glass measuring cup to weigh out your ingredients accurately. Just because I haven't listed these items every time, they are still necessary, so if you don't have an oven, please borrow one before getting started.

5) A handy kit tip: a baking pan has a rim or short sides, while a cookie sheet hasn't.

6) In recipes, there are a number of terms used regularly that aren't always self-explanatory. Believe it or not, you don't need a blindfold to blind bake pastry and knocking back is not just something you do with tequila. To avoid confusion (and for your own safety/sobriety), I have included a handy Glossary of Cooking Terms on pages 9–11. Give it a read before getting started on the recipes and know it is there to refer back to, should you need it. If nothing else, you'll end up feeling oh-so-knowledgeable and may just find yourself killing it the next time a baking question pops up during your pub quiz. Cooking terms that feature in the glossary are written in **bold** in the recipes, so you know at a glance which ones are covered.

7) I use whole (full-fat) EVERYTHING. And so should you. Especially for baking. Please assume, unless specified otherwise, all dairy products (milk, cream, butter, cream cheese, cheese…) are undeniably that.

8) Eggs. Free-range please. Very important to me. And assume size "Large" unless stated otherwise.

9) If you can't locate superfine sugar at your grocer's, you can make your own with a food processor. It's best to follow instructions found on the internet so you come out with the proper amount, and so you don't end up with a kitchen coated in more sugar dust than your bake.

10) Some of my methods might not be the most traditional, technical, or efficient, but they work for me, so I'm hoping they'll work for you too. If not, maybe you'll develop your own way of doing things. This isn't a patisserie book with set rules to follow. So do what you have to do to get the result you need.

11) I want to know how you get on, so please share your bakes with me by tagging me on Instagram, DMing me photos, and using the hashtag #bakingimperfect. The bakes don't even have to be from this book; I would just like to see what you're up to.

SHOW ME YOUR BAKES
@LOTTIEGOTCAKE
I WANNA SEE!

Glossary of Cooking Terms

Bain-marie A cooking technique whereby food is heated gently in a heatproof bowl or pan placed over or in a pan of simmering water. Most commonly this method is used to melt chocolate by placing it in a heatproof bowl over a saucepan of simmering water on the burner (without the base of the bowl touching the water). However, if you have a microwave, you may find it easier and quicker to melt chocolate using my **heat, stir, repeat** method (see page 10). In the puddings chapter of this book, you will also use a bain-marie in the oven to cook my Ginger & Rhubarb Puddings, Peanut Butter & Jam Roly-Poly, and Lemon & Raspberry Soufflé. Steamy stuff.

Basting By cooking meat in its own juices (and lots of butter), you stop it from drying out. Tilt the pan slightly toward you, fill a spoon with the juice, tip it over the meat, and repeat and repeat and repeat.

Blind bake This really is key when trying to avoid a "soggy bottom." By lining your unbaked pastry with foil or parchment paper and then topping with pie weights or dried lentils or rice (anything heavy enough to weigh the paper down), you are ensuring that the pastry is baked thoroughly before adding your filling. This also prevents the pastry crust from puffing up in the oven or shrinking away from the sides. When you have blind baked, it is always important to remove the weights and bake, uncovered, for another few minutes to crisp up the crust. On smaller pastry bakes, you might be able to get away without blind baking— a matter of trial and error really.

Bloom Before you use gelatin (in sheet or powder form) to thicken something or make a gelatin dessert, you need to bloom it, which is really easy to do. Put the gelatin into a little liquid and let stand for 3 to 5 minutes. Once heated, the gelatin will melt and dissolve evenly into whatever you're making.

Cook out When making a sauce or choux pastry, the flour needs to cook so that there isn't a floury taste in the finished bake. When your mixture fizzes and starts to leave a white coating on the bottom of the pan, you know that the flour is cooking and you can continue on to the next step.

Cream This is a fantastic dairy product but also a method of combining butter and sugar together until "light and fluffy." But what does that actually look like? Butter doesn't really look strokeable and fluffy no matter how much you cream it. What it actually means is getting the butter and sugar to a stage where the color is paler and the sugar is dissolved into the butter. The mixture will increase in volume and result in airy bakes. Your butter needs to be room temperature to cream most effectively. Be like me and have sticks of butter on every windowsill just in case you need to cream some.

Crimping The many options for sealing the edges of a pasty or other pastry items, the simplest being pressing down with the prongs of a fork.

Dropping consistency Refers to when the mixture is of the texture that will drop from your whisk and back into the bowl. When the mixture drops from the spoon/paddle/whisk, you want it to form a "V" shape.

Egg, separated There are many recipes in this book that require either just the white or just the yolk of an egg. To separate, crack the egg and then cradle the contents back and forth either between the shell halves or your hands so that just the yolk is remaining and the white is caught in a bowl under your hands. When whisking egg whites, it is really important that there is no yolk in them at all, so it is worth taking a little extra time in the cradling to make sure you don't pierce the yolk.

Egg wash I've included this because I don't like the mystery around the phrase. It is a beaten egg or two that is brushed onto pastry to make it golden brown. Some people put milk in there. I don't.

Fold When you are mixing ingredients together, folding ensures you don't knock the air out of the existing mixture. Using a spatula or spoon, you lift the mixture from underneath and move it to the top, repeating until the added ingredient is incorporated.

Heat, stir, repeat While you can always melt chocolate using a **bain-marie** on the burner (see page 9), you can also cheat and use a microwave. Break the chocolate up and put in a microwave-safe bowl, heat it for 30 seconds, stir it, and repeat until melted. How long this takes will depend on the quantity of chocolate you are melting at one time. Any longer than 30-second intervals and you risk burning the chocolate. When it is nearly melted with a few lumps remaining, use the residual heat of the bowl and stir vigorously to encourage the final bits to melt.

Knead When you knead a dough, you're trying to promote elasticity in the gluten, i.e., you want to stretch it. I do this using the heel of my hands to elongate it and push it away from me before rolling it back toward me, rotating a little, and then repeating.

Knock back Once a dough has had its first **prove**, before the shaping stage, you want to knock the air out of it so that it is encouraged to re-form again in the shape you want. You can punch it, poke it, **knead** it—whatever you want. It might make little squeaking noises when you knock it back, but that's just the air escaping. This will make the dough small again but, don't worry, the second prove will sort that out.

Lamination Found within my rough puff pastry recipe (see page 129), this is the process of layering butter onto your pastry, folding it, and then continuing to do so to create butter/pastry layers. These layers then crisp up in the oven to form buttery and flaky pastry.

Pipe I am not one for intricate decoration, but sometimes using a pastry bag can actually make life easier. For example, if you are trying to fill profiteroles, squirting the filling in with a pastry bag is way more effective than using a spoon. Trust me, I've tried. When it comes to choosing a pastry bag, you can get rubbery reusable ones or disposable ones that are recyclable once rinsed. The latter is my preference because I can never get the rubber ones truly clean. Tips are a whole other topic; you can buy thousands of different shapes and sizes. Google "Russian Tips" to blow your mind and see what's possible. As far as I'm concerned, you can't go wrong with a Wilton 2D for piping cupcakes or flowery splodges and an additional narrow, plain tip for filling, or decorating

cookies. Just open the bag, drop the tip in until it sits at the pointed end, fill, and then snip the end of the bag and squeeze the tip into place. If you don't have a tip handy, just snip the end of the pastry bag to suit the size you want to pipe, so the lower down to the corner you snip, the thinner the piping, the further up the bag, the larger the hole so the thicker the piping. Riveting stuff. Filling a pastry bag can be a messy, sticky business. If you don't have a second pair of hands to help, put the bag in a 16-ounce glass, roll the top down over the rim, and then fill it. This holds the bag steady in an upright position and stops the majority ending up on the outside of the bag.

Prove When yeasted dough is left in a warm place, the yeast feeds on starches in the flour and creates air bubbles that make the dough rise or "double in size" as they say. This process is called proving. First prove is, as it sounds, the first time you let the dough rise. Second prove is after you have shaped the dough and you let it rise for a second time.

Reduce Reducing a liquid describes the process of heating it until it is boiling and begins to reduce in volume. This is normally done to intensify the flavor of the liquid and thicken it by removing some of the water content.

Ribbon stage This describes the texture and thickness of a whisked egg and (most often) sugar mixture. When you lift the whisk out of the mixture, the "ribbons" of mixture will be thick enough, once they have fallen from the whisk back into the bowl, to remain visible on the surface before slowly disappearing back into the mixture. You can also try drawing a figure eight with the mixture. If you complete the "8" without it sinking, it's ready to go!

Shoot the flour I have no idea where this saying comes from, but I remember Prue Leith saying it to me in the *Bake Off* tent, so I know it's a thing. When you're making choux pastry (see page 126) and you add the flour to the butter and water, lots of recipes call for the flour to be sifted and placed on a piece of parchment paper that is folded in half and then tipped into the saucepan all at once, as quickly as possible. No idea if it makes for a smoother choux, but what Prue says, goes.

Soft peaks When whisking cream or egg whites and you remove the whisk, the mixture should peak but barely hold its shape and flop over at the top. Don't hold this one over your head. Without filming it.

Split In this book, split will most likely be referring to cream (not banana, sorry). When you overwhip cream, past the **stiff peaks** stage, it will split and separate. If this happens, you can experiment by whisking in more milk or cream, but don't feel bad if you need to start again. Interesting fact: were you to keep whisking the split cream, you would eventually end up with cloudy water (buttermilk) and clumps which, if squished together and rinsed, would form butter.

Stiff peaks When you're whisking cream or egg whites and you remove the whisk, the mixture left behind in the bowl should peak and stand up straight. This is also the stage at which you see people holding bowls over their heads to test the firmness of their whisking. Risky whisking.

Tempering When you buy a bar of chocolate, it has been tempered. This is what makes it snap when you break it or bite into it. When you melt chocolate to decorate something or try to make shapes with it, if you don't temper it, it will be dull, never fully set at room temperature, and will bend instead of snap. So it's worth doing.

I temper using the "seeding" method because life is too short and I don't have the surface space to do it the traditional way. To temper like you mean it, you do need a sugar thermometer. Take one-third of the chocolate you are using, finely chop, and set aside. Melt the remaining chocolate using the **heat, stir, repeat** method and check the temperature. The "working" temperature of chocolate depends on the percentage of cocoa solids it contains: 122–131°F for dark (semi-sweet) chocolate; 113–122°F for milk or white chocolate. Once it has reached the correct working temperature, add a small amount of the finely chopped chocolate you set aside earlier and stir vigorously until it melts. Add some more of the chopped chocolate and stir again until melted. This will gradually bring the temperature of the chocolate down. For dark (semi-sweet) chocolate, you are looking to reach 88–89°F, for milk 81–82°F, and for

white chocolate 83–84°F. If the chocolate cools too much, heat it back up and start again with more chocolate, but just remember that you need to add one-third of the total quantity of chocolate when seeding.

Well, to make a When you are mixing flour and wet ingredients, it is sometimes easier to make a well in the flour first. This is simply making an indent in the middle of the flour and pouring the wet ingredients into it. To combine, stir the wet ingredients, gradually picking up flour from the sides and incorporating it.

Windowpane test Making dough involves kneading. A LOT of kneading. To test whether it is ready to prove, you can pull off a small piece of the dough and stretch it. If it breaks before you've had a chance to stretch it fully, then you need to **knead** more. Holding it up to the light, you should be able to see your fingers through the stretched dough, hence the name.

Zest This is both a noun and a verb. Zesting a citrus fruit is easiest with a Microplane but can also be done on a regular grater. Always try and buy "unwaxed" fruit where possible and take just the colored skin off the fruit, leaving the white pith behind. The pith is bitter. If you can't buy unwxaed fruit, pour recently boiled water over the fruit and give them a good scrub before zesting.

For beginners and people who generally have less time to mess around, cookies and biscuits are often seen as a good way into baking. There are some simple cookie bakes in this chapter that will leave you with something just as nice as a gigantic cake that takes a whole day of your life to make (though if that's your thing, please see pages 78–81). There are also snacky cookies for eating whenever, as well as fancy cookies for when an important visitor, like the Queen, comes around for afternoon tea. There are cookies for adults with flavors like spiced rum, and great options for kids, such as the Chocolate & Raspberry Pinwheels (see pages 17–18). My signature, handshake-worthy Quarantine Florentines make an appearance too (see pages 14–16).

I hope you can use this chapter to get confident with some useful skills that will appear further on in the book, like stewing fruit, piping decorations, and making caramel. Just remember not to sweat the small stuff. No one cares what they look like if they taste good.

Difficulty:

Quarantine Florentines

I've been baking cookies for my grandparents for as long as I can remember, and these are their favorites. They're irresistible, so don't let any go to waste. You can even use the offcuts as a naughty breakfast cereal the next day. And if there are nuts or dried fruits I haven't included but you want to get in there, go for it. Make this one your own.

KIT LIST
2 baking pans
small food processor
round cookie cutter

For the cookies
⅓ cup pistachio nuts
½ cup dried sour cherries
¼ cup crystallized ginger
2½ tablespoons all-purpose flour
½ cup coconut flakes
1⅓ cups sliced almonds
½ stick unsalted butter
½ cup firmly packed light brown sugar
pinch of salt
2 to 3 tablespoons heavy cream

To decorate
6 ounces dark (semi-sweet) chocolate
   (54% cocoa solids minimum), broken
   into pieces
2¾ ounces white chocolate, broken
   into pieces

1 Preheat the oven to 375°F and line the baking pans with parchment paper. Put the pistachios, cherries, and ginger into a small food processor and blitz for a few seconds until chopped to a fine rubble. Add the flour and blitz again to combine. Transfer the mixture to a bowl and stir in the coconut flakes and sliced almonds.

2 Heat the butter, sugar, and salt in a small saucepan over low heat, without stirring if possible but moving the pan around to combine, until the sugar has melted and the mixture is a darker golden brown. Remove from the heat and stir in the cream. Pour this caramel over the fruit mixture and stir until well combined.

3 Place 1 tablespoon of the mixture on one of the lined baking pans and press it out to an even thickness. Use the cookie cutter to help guide you here if needed. Don't worry about holes in the mixture because, when it cooks, the caramel will melt and fill the gaps. Repeat until you have 6 circles of mixture on each baking pan, with plenty of room in between to allow for spreading during baking. If you run out of room on the baking sheets, bake in batches.* Bake for 8 to 10 minutes, or until evenly golden brown. Watch them carefully. If they are paler in the center, they may be a little softer and chewy to eat; if they are overbrowned, they will be too snappy. It's a fine line, so keep a close eye on them.

*Even with some room between them, you might find that the Florentines still merge together into one big blob. That's not an issue at all because we are going to use a cookie cutter later on anyway, so just keep going and adjust the shape further down the line.

WAIT, THERE'S MORE...

4 Remove from the oven and let cool on the baking pans until hard. Transfer the Florentines to a wire rack, then line the baking sheets again with parchment paper and place in the freezer**.

5 Using the cookie cutter, stamp out the cookies on a flat surface into neat, round shapes. Return to the wire rack to cool completely.

6 Meanwhile, melt the dark chocolate in a microwave-safe bowl in the microwave using the **heat, stir, repeat** method until smooth. Remove the baking pans from the freezer. Dip the base of each Florentine in the melted chocolate, then press the cookies, chocolate side-down, on your ice-cold lined baking pans. If you press too hard you will crack the cookies, but you should be pressing hard enough that some chocolate squishes up through the holes.

7 While the dark chocolate sets, melt the white chocolate in the same way. Drizzle it over the dark chocolate—get creative. Let stand to set.

✳✳
Freezing the pans will help set the melted chocolate quicker once the cookies have been dipped.

Store in an airtight container in a cool place for up to 3 days, or until they lose their snap.

Difficulty:

Chocolate & Raspberry Pinwheels

GIVE THEM A WHIRL

I don't know what to tell you about these cookies other than they're pink and brown and they go round and round. And they look cool. This recipe is simple, but the assembly can be fiddly. What I'm trying to say is, don't stress about the shape, as the flavors will taste good regardless.

KIT LIST
food processor
toothpick
baking pan

For the cookies
2 cups all-purpose flour, plus extra for
    dusting
1⅓ sticks unsalted butter, softened
1 large egg, beaten
½ cup superfine sugar
½ teaspoon salt
½ teaspoon vanilla bean paste
⅛ teaspoon raspberry extract
pink gel food coloring
2¾ ounces dark (semi-sweet) chocolate
    (54% cocoa solids minimum), broken
    into pieces
9 ounces milk chocolate, broken into pieces

To decorate
freeze-dried raspberry pieces
raspberry powder

1 Blitz the flour and butter together in a food processor until the mixture looks like large breadcrumbs. Add the egg, sugar, salt, and vanilla paste, and briefly blitz again until large lumps start to form. Lightly flour a work surface, turn the mixture out onto it, and bring together with your hands into a dough. (Be careful not to overwork it here. Just do enough to form it into a solid ball). Halve the dough with a knife.

2 Add the raspberry extract to one half of the dough along with a little food coloring—I dip a toothpick in to pick up a pea-sized amount. Using your hands, work the coloring through the dough until you have a ball that is an even pink with no streaks.

3 Melt the dark chocolate in a microwave-safe bowl in the microwave using the **heat, stir, repeat** method until smooth, then let cool. Add to the other half of the dough, a little at a time, working it though until it is uniformly brown (you may want to do this in a bowl).

4 Wrap both balls of dough separately in plastic wrap and let chill in the fridge for at least an hour.

WAIT, THERE'S MORE...

5 Lay out a large piece of plastic wrap on your work surface. Remove both doughs from the fridge. Unwrap the raspberry dough first, and place it in the center of the fresh piece of plastic wrap. Use a rolling pin to roll it out into the biggest rectangle you can without the dough ripping or sticking to the surface (it should be about 1/16 inch thick).* Repeat the process with the chocolate dough on a separate piece of plastic wrap.

6 Carefully and quickly, pick up the chocolate dough, still on the plastic wrap, and flip it on top of the raspberry dough. Peel off the plastic wrap from the chocolate dough and then trim the edges to make sure your doughs now form one neat rectangle.

7 Start at one of the shorter edges of the rectangle. Using the plastic wrap beneath the raspberry dough to help you, roll up the combined dough into a tight sausage shape. Tighten the plastic wrap around the sausage ends and refrigerate for 40 minutes.

8 Preheat the oven to 350°F and line a baking pan with parchment paper. Remove the dough sausage from the fridge and cut into 16 slices. Place your slices on the lined baking pan, leaving a couple of inches between each to allow for spreading during baking. Bake for 12 to 15 minutes. Remove from the oven and transfer the pinwheels to a wire rack to cool completely.

9 Melt the milk chocolate in the same way as you did the dark chocolate in step 3. Lower one face of each cookie into the melted chocolate and scrape off any excess drippage. Return, chocolate-side up, to the wire rack, then sprinkle with freeze-dried raspberry pieces and dust with raspberry powder (be careful, a little goes a long way). Let them set before serving.

✳ Don't get overexcited and take the dough out of the fridge too soon. If it's too warm, it will rip and stick to the rolling pin, generally making your life a misery. If this does happen, smush the dough back together and return to the fridge. It should feel cold to the touch before you get going.

 Store in an airtight container in a cool place for up to 3 days.

Gingerbread Whoopie Pies with Pineapple & Spiced Rum

WHOOPSIE-DAISY I ADDED TOO MUCH RUM

This recipe is an excuse to stick cookies together with loads of filling. The whoopie pie isn't traditional because it's made with gingerbread, so it's soft and chewy. Feel free to make it as spicy as you can handle.

KIT LIST
cookie sheet
food processor or electric hand mixer
pastry bag

For the pineapple filling
2 tablespoons unsalted butter
1½ cups diced fresh pineapple
2 tablespoons soft light brown sugar
¼ cup spiced rum

For the cookies
⅔ stick unsalted butter
½ cup firmly packed soft light brown sugar
⅓ cup firmly packed soft dark brown sugar
1 tablespoon light corn syrup
2¼ cups all-purpose flour
1½ teaspoons baking soda
1½ teaspoons ground ginger
¼ teaspoon ground cinnamon
pinch of ground nutmeg
1 egg, beaten

For the buttercream filling
1 stick unsalted butter
½ cup powdered sugar
2 teaspoons vanilla bean paste

1 Preheat the oven to 350°F and line a cookie sheet with parchment paper.

2 To make the pineapple filling, add the butter, pineapple, and brown sugar to a large skillet and cook over medium heat until soft and sticky. Add the rum and let simmer over low heat for 10 minutes until **reduced**, stirring to ensure it doesn't burn. Set aside to cool.

3 To make the cookies, heat the butter, sugars, and light corn syrup in a medium saucepan over medium heat until the sugars have melted, stirring to stop them from burning. Sift the flour, baking soda, and spices together into a large bowl, then pour in the butter mixture, stirring to combine. Add the egg and stir.

4 Using your hands, roll the dough into balls weighing about 1 ounce each. You'll need an even number of balls so you can sandwich them together later. Place on the lined cookie sheet, leaving a little space in between to allow for spreading during baking. Bake for 7 to 8 minutes. Remove from the oven and let cool completely on the cookie sheet (they will harden as they cool, so don't worry if they feel squishy).

5 Meanwhile, to make the buttercream filling, blitz the butter, powdered sugar, and vanilla paste together in a food processor, or beat together in a bowl with an electric hand mixer. Transfer to a pastry bag.

WAIT, THERE'S MORE... ➡

 Store in an airtight container in a cool place for up to 2 days.

✳ If you squish the cookies together with too much force, your buttercream might smush out of the sides, which would be sad. If this does happen, carefully scrape off or scoop up the escaped filling and return whatever you can rescue to the pastry bag for take 2. Next time, be more gentle! The buttercream will hold the 2 halves of your pie together without your brute force.

6 Pipe a border of buttercream onto the flat side of each cooled cookie, going over it a couple of times to ensure a nice amount of filling. Then fill the hole with pineapple and sandwich two cookies together.*

Difficulty:

Triple Chocolate & Salted Caramel-Centered Cookies

ABSOLUTE FILTH

If you don't have a sweet tooth, then this isn't the cookie for you. There's absolutely no need for this to be triple chocolate and caramel. It might even be a bit much, but I did it anyway. You're welcome.

KIT LIST
food processor
cookie sheet
stand mixer or electric hand mixer
baking pan
rubber spatula
metal spatula (optional)

For the cookies
2¾ ounces milk chocolate
2¾ ounces dark (semi-sweet) chocolate (54% cocoa solids minimum)
2¾ ounces white chocolate
1 stick unsalted butter, softened
½ cup firmly packed soft light brown sugar
¼ cup superfine sugar
1 egg
1¾ cups all-purpose flour
3 tablespoons unsweetened cocoa powder
½ teaspoon baking powder
¼ teaspoon salt
glass of milk, to serve (optional)

For the caramel centers
½ stick unsalted butter
1½ tablespoons light corn syrup
1 tablespoon superfine sugar
½ cup condensed milk

1 For the cookies, break up the three kinds of chocolate into a food processor and blitz to rubble. Don't worry if there are some bigger chunks than others.

2 Line a cookie sheet with parchment paper. **Cream** the butter and sugars together in a stand mixer or in a large bowl with an electric hand mixer. Add the egg and beat in. Sift in the flour, cocoa powder, baking powder, and salt, then **fold** in. Mix in the chocolate rubble.

3 Bring the dough together with your hands in the bowl, then tear off pieces weighing about 1½ ounces each, and roll them into balls. You'll need an even number of balls so you can sandwich them together later. You're dealing with a lot of chocolate here, so if your hands are too warm, your dough might get a bit melty and wet. But just keep going and lick your hands when you're done. Put your balls on the lined cookie sheet and pop them (uncovered) in the fridge for an hour.

4 Halfway through the dough chilling time, preheat the oven to 350°F and begin making the caramel centers. Heat the butter, light corn syrup, and sugar in a medium saucepan over medium heat and stir until the butter has melted. Bring to a gentle boil and continue boiling, stirring constantly, for about 3 to 5 minutes until the sugar has melted (when you press a spatula against the side of the pan, you shouldn't feel any sugar crystals) and the mixture has just started to darken. Add the condensed milk and stir vigorously for another 15 minutes, making sure no mixture is sticking to the bottom or sides of the pan. By this time the caramel will have thickened and, if you have stirred it well, it will have a smooth consistency. If there are little brown flecks, fear not—it will taste the same, but your stirring needs work for next time.

WAIT, THERE'S MORE...

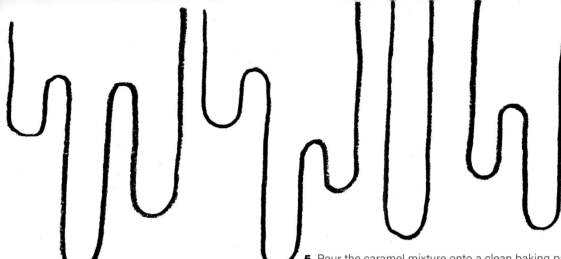

5 Pour the caramel mixture onto a clean baking pan (don't worry about it sticking to the bottom). Spread out with a spatula, then let cool.

6 Once their chilling time is up, remove your dough balls from the fridge, pick up your first, and then press into it with your thumb to create a small indentation. Scoop a ball of cooled caramel from the baking pan and fit it into the indentation. Now sandwich this with another dough ball and then roll them together in your hands to give the ball a smooth finish. (You want the caramel completely covered by an outer coating of smooth dough to make sure there is minimal leakage when baking.) Return to the lined cookie sheet, then repeat with your remaining dough balls, leaving a sizable gap in between each to allow for spreading during baking.

7 Bake for 15 minutes. Remove from the oven and let cool for a few minutes on the cookie sheet before transferring to a wire rack to cool completely. Don't move them too soon or the caramel will plop straight out the bottom and the whole thing will fall apart.* These are good heated in the microwave and enjoyed with a glass of milk.

* If you've taken the cookies out of the oven and you notice that the outside edge is looking a little cracked or dry, wait for them to cool slightly, then take a round cookie cutter and use it to cut a large circle out of the middle. Dispose of the offcuts in your mouth or the trash.

Store in an airtight container in a cool place for up to 3 days.

Difficulty:

Millionaire Shortbread with Boozy Ganache

FOR WHEN TOO MUCH JUST ISN'T ENOUGH

Whatever too much is, this is more than that. Using my fail-safe (I think) caramel method, this recipe throws chocolate chips into the shortbread and liqueur into the ganache. It's definitely a marathon not a sprint, so not one to make in a hurry. There are several stages and you'll have to show determination to make it from start to finish. Worth it though.

KIT LIST
12-inch x 9-inch brownie pan or 9-inch square loose-bottomed baking pan
food processor
rubber spatula
large pastry bag (optional)
toothpick (optional)

For the shortbread base
1¾ cups all-purpose flour
1¼ sticks unsalted butter, softened
⅓ cup superfine sugar
⅓ cup milk chocolate chips

For the caramel
¾ stick unsalted butter
3½ tablespoons light corn syrup
3 tablespoons superfine sugar
14-ounce can condensed milk

For the ganache
½ cup heavy cream
7 ounces dark (semi-sweet) chocolate (54% cocoa solids minimum)
2 fluid ounces Irish cream liqueur (I use Baileys)

For the topping
5½ ounces milk chocolate, broken into small pieces
1¾ ounces white chocolate, broken into small pieces

To make the shortbread base

1 Preheat the oven to 350°F and line your baking pan with parchment paper.

2 Put all the ingredients for the shortbread base apart from the chocolate chips into a food processor and blitz to a dough. Transfer to a bowl, then work the chocolate chips evenly through the dough using your hands or a spatula. Transfer the dough to the lined pan and press it out flat to cover the base, making sure it reaches right into the corners and is as even as possible (the back of a spoon might help you here). Bake for 25 minutes.

3 Remove from the oven and let cool in the pan.

To make the caramel

4 While the base is baking, heat the butter, light corn syrup, and sugar in a medium saucepan over medium heat. Bring to a gentle boil and continue boiling, stirring constantly, until the butter and sugar have melted (when you press a spatula against the side of the pan, you shouldn't feel any sugar crystals) and the mixture has darkened (this normally takes about 8 minutes for me). Add the condensed milk and stir for another 15 minutes, making sure no mixture is sticking to the bottom or sides of the pan.

5 You will now have a fudgy-textured caramel. Pour this straight onto the cooling shortbread base in the pan and let cool to room temperature before chilling in the fridge for an hour.

WAIT, THERE'S MORE...

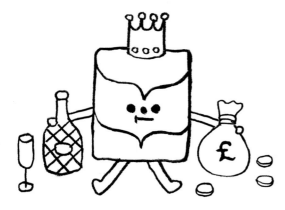

To make the ganache

6 Heat the cream in a small saucepan over low heat until steaming but not boiling. While the cream is heating, break up the chocolate into small pieces and place in a large heatproof bowl. Pour the hot cream over the chocolate, making sure all of it is covered, and let stand for about 5 minutes to melt before stirring vigorously to form a smooth chocolatey cream.* Splash in the booze and stir again. Pour the ganache on top of the chilled caramel and smooth out as much as possible, then return to the fridge for an hour to set.

To add the topping

7 Melt the milk chocolate in a microwave-safe bowl in the microwave using the **heat, stir, repeat** method. Do the same with the white chocolate in a separate microwave-safe bowl. Pour the melted chocolates on top of the chilled ganache layer in any pattern you like. (I pour the milk chocolate on first and then **pipe** the white chocolate on in lines and drag a toothpick through it to create traditional feathering.) Chill in the fridge for 30 minutes before carving and serving. Use a hot knife to cut your slices and make them small. You don't need much of this!

✳ If you've stirred vigorously for some time, the mixture has cooled, and you still haven't lost all of the chocolate lumps, then you'll need to play a risky game with the microwave. This mixture MUST NOT get too warm, so pop your bowl in for 10 seconds MAXIMUM and stir as quickly as you can to get rid of those lumps once and for all.

 Store in the fridge for up to 3 days.

Difficulty:

Chocolate-Dipped Ginger Cookies

ONE FOR THE GROWN-UPS, IF YOU KNOW ANY

You couldn't call me sophisticated (and I gave up trying a long time ago), but these cookies have some pretty mature flavors going on. The fiery ginger and dark chocolate make them perfect to enjoy by themselves, but you could also use them for the base of a cheesecake (such as my Mango & Grapefruit Crème Brûlée Cheesecake on pages 69–70).

KIT LIST
stand mixer or electric hand mixer
rubber spatula (optional)
cookie sheet

Ingredients
½ stick unsalted butter, softened
¼ cup firmly packed soft light brown sugar
2½ tablespoons light corn syrup
1 egg
1½ cups all-purpose flour
½ teaspoon baking soda
3 teaspoons ground ginger
½ teaspoon ground cinnamon
pinch of salt
3½ ounces dark (semi-sweet) chocolate
  (54% cocoa solids minimum)

1 Cream the butter, sugar, and light corn syrup together in a stand mixer or in a bowl with an electric hand mixer. Add the egg and beat in. Sift in the flour, baking soda, spices, and salt and mix until combined.

2 Lay out a piece of plastic wrap on your work surface and transfer the mixture onto it, then wrap and chill in the fridge for an hour.

3 Preheat the oven to 350°F and line a cookie sheet with parchment paper.

4 Roll the dough into balls about the size of a ping-pong ball. Place the balls on the lined cookie sheet and flatten them slightly, leaving a walnut-sized gap between each. Bake for 12 to 15 minutes. Remove from the oven and transfer the cookies to a wire rack to cool completely.

5 Meanwhile, melt the chocolate in a microwave-safe bowl using the **heat, stir, repeat method**.

6 Dip the cooled cookies into the melted chocolate or drizzle the chocolate. Basically, you can do what you want with the chocolate. Let set before serving.

 Store in an airtight container at room temperature for up to 3 days.

Whiskey Snaps

THEY'RE PRETTY NEAT...

Everyone has heard of brandy snaps (served with ice cream in pubs everywhere here in the UK), but who has heard of whiskey snaps? I'm hoping nobody, because I'm fairly confident that this is a genius idea. I don't like brandy, but I do like whiskey.

KIT LIST
2 baking pans
hand whisk
ovenproof bowl or cannoli tubes,
  or similar-shaped items for molding

Ingredients
3½ tablespoons unsalted butter
¼ cup superfine sugar
2½ tablespoons light corn syrup
pinch of salt
1 teaspoon fresh orange juice
1 tablespoon whiskey
½ cup all-purpose flour
½ teaspoon ground ginger
ice cream or mousse, to serve

1 Preheat the oven to 350°F and line the baking pans with parchment paper.

2 Heat the butter, sugar, light corn syrup, salt, orange juice, and whiskey in a medium saucepan over medium heat until the sugar has dissolved, stirring to stop it from burning. Remove from the heat and let cool slightly. Then add the flour and ginger and whisk with a hand whisk until smooth and no lumps remain.

3 Place 1 tablespoon of the mixture on one of the lined baking pans, then use the back of the tablespoon to spread it out, using a circular motion, until evenly spread in a circle. Repeat until you have 4 disks on the baking pan with a large gap in between to allow for spreading during baking. Repeat with the remaining mixture (you may have to do 3 or 4 batches).

4 Bake for 9 minutes, then remove from the oven. The disks should look lacy and delicate. As soon as they are just cool enough for you to touch, mold them around little ovenproof bowls or cannoli tubes to create a cup shape.*

5 Let cool completely, then fill with ice cream or mousse to serve.

 Store in an airtight container at room temperature for up to 2 days.

✳ The snaps might start to rip and tear when you try to mold them into their shapes. This can look like a disaster, but it's really not. Put the baking pan back into the oven, trying to keep the disks in their circular shape, and bake for a couple more minutes. When you take them out, let them cool for a bit longer than you did the first time. The idea is that they are firm enough to hold their form, but not so tough that they can't be shaped. Worst-case scenario, you are left with lots of shattered bits of whiskey snaps. Sprinkle them on your ice cream instead.

Rhubarb & Custard Sandwich Cookies

THE HOLY GRAIL OF MY COOKIE LIST

These are kind of like the rhubarb and custard version of that famous British biscuit I can't mention that has jam in the middle and rhymes with hammy roger. I should warn you that they're an absolute nightmare to eat, so don't get them out in front of anyone you're trying to flirt with or impress. The filling gets everywhere!

KIT LIST
food processor
2 pastry bags
2¾-inch round cookie cutter
smaller round cookie cutter, about 1¼ inches
   (if you don't have this, use a bottle top)
2 cookie sheets

For the cookies
2 cups all-purpose flour, plus 2½ tablespoons
   for dusting
1 stick unsalted butter, cubed and chilled
⅓ cup superfine sugar
1 large egg
1 teaspoon vanilla bean paste
pinch of salt

For the fillings
2½ cups chopped rhubarb, (chop the
   pieces to about ½ inch in size)
1 tablespoon superfine sugar
3 teaspoons gelling sugar
pink gel food coloring (optional)
1 stick unsalted butter, softened
¾ cup powdered sugar
2 teaspoons instant custard powder or
   instant vanilla pudding mix
1½ teaspoons vanilla bean paste

1 To make the cookies, blitz the flour, butter, and sugar together in a food processor until the mixture looks like fine breadcrumbs. Beat the egg and vanilla paste together in a large bowl, then mix in the flour mixture and salt. It will look very crumbly at first, but use your hands to work the mixture together into a dough. Wrap in plastic wrap and let chill in the fridge for an hour.

2 Meanwhile, make the fillings. Put the rhubarb into a medium saucepan with a splash of water. Add the sugars, heat until just simmering, stirring occasionally, and cook until soft. Taste to check the sourness. If it's too sour, add a little more sugar, but remember this is being put in a sweet cookie with a custard buttercream, so don't overdo it! Let the rhubarb cool and then blitz in your food processor until smooth. Add a small blob of pink coloring, if you want to, and stir through. (The coloring is totally optional, but depending on the season, your rhubarb might not be all that pink, so it's good to have as backup just in case.) Set aside to cool, then transfer to a pastry bag and place in the fridge.

3 For the buttercream, blitz the remaining ingredients (butter, powdered sugar, custard powder, and vanilla paste) in your food processor, then transfer to another pastry bag and set aside.*

 Store in an airtight container at room temperature for up to 2 days.

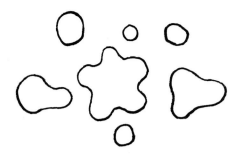

4 Preheat the oven to 350°F. Lay a large piece of parchment paper on your work surface. Remove the dough from the fridge, unwrap it, and place it in the center of the paper. Dust half the additional flour on the parchment paper around the dough and on the dough itself. Squash the dough down a little to make it flat, then top with a second piece of parchment paper. Use a rolling pin to gently roll out the dough to a thickness of about ⅛ inch. Peel off the top piece of paper and, using the larger cookie cutter, stamp out 10 circles. Remove and gather together the leftover dough to leave just the circles on the parchment paper, then transfer, still on the paper, to a cookie sheet.

5 Repeat the rolling-out process with the gathered-up dough and remaining flour, then stamp out another 10 circles for the tops. Transfer these to the second cookie sheet, then use the smaller cutter to cut out a hole in the center of each. Bake for 10 minutes, then remove from the oven. When cool enough to handle, transfer to a wire rack to cool completely.

6 Pipe a border of buttercream around the edge of each whole cookie, then pipe a border line down the center and fill in one side with buttercream. Fill the remaining half with rhubarb. Top with a holey cookie and gently squish it on top.

✳ If your room is particularly warm, you may want to put the buttercream in the fridge while you make the cookies. When ready to use, just warm it with your hands until it is pipeable.

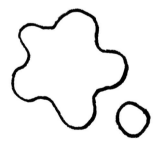

PIPE, SPOON, SQUISH, SCOFF... ➤ ➤

Gibbo's Garibaldis (Dead Fly Cookies)

I CAN'T LIE. THESE AREN'T MY FAVORITE.

I don't really like these, but I wrote the recipe for a friend who is very pleased with them, so I'm fairly confident it works. They're a good snack to have around, maybe even part of your five-a-day thanks to all the dried fruit. The turbinado is crucial to the crunch, so don't swap it out for superfine unless you must. Good luck with the rolling.

KIT LIST
rubber spatula (optional)
cookie sheet
pastry brush

Ingredients
1 stick unsalted butter, softened
⅓ cup superfine sugar
1 egg, beaten
1⅔ cups all-purpose flour
pinch of salt
¼ cup dried blueberries, finely chopped
¼ cup dried cherries, finely chopped
1 egg white, beaten
turbinado sugar, for sprinkling on top

1 Cream the butter and sugar together in a bowl with a wooden spoon, then gradually beat in the whole egg. Sift in the flour and salt, then stir until combined. Stir in the dried fruit, then bring the dough together with your hands in the bowl.

2 Lay a large piece of parchment paper on your work surface. Place your dough in the center, then top with another piece of parchment paper. Roll out the dough into a rough rectangle to fit the dimensions of your cookie sheet and about 1⁄16 inch in thickness. If your cookie sheet is too small to fit the dough rectangle at this thickness, separate the dough into 2 or 3 lumps and proceed with rolling out and making the cookies in batches. It's important that the dough is this thin, so don't worry if it seems fragile. Once it's rolled out, peel off the top piece of paper and trim your edges to make a neater rectangle.

3 Using a sharp knife, score (don't cut all the way through) the rectangle in half lengthwise. Next, score 7 equally spaced lines from top to bottom across both halves, resulting in 16 smaller rectangles (still only scored, not cut). Transfer the whole rectangle, with the remaining parchment paper, onto a cookie sheet and let chill in the fridge for 30 minutes.

4 Preheat the oven to 350°F, and then bake the cookies for 10 minutes.

5 Remove from the oven, then use a pastry brush to brush the tops of the cookies with the egg white and sprinkle with turbinado sugar. Bake for another 8 minutes, or until golden brown. Let the cookies cool on the cookie sheet before transferring to a wire rack. They should easily snap apart along the scored lines.*

✳ If the cookies don't snap easily into the rectangles, push a knife very gently into the score line. It really shouldn't need much force and you don't want them to shatter. But then again, it's fine if they do.

 Store in an airtight container at room temperature for up to 3 days.

Difficulty:

Baba's Gluten-Free Biscotti

THIS ONE'S NOT FOR LOTTIE

Every half-decent baking book needs at least one gluten-free recipe, so here's mine. (And it turns out this can be dairy-free too.) This is inspired by a recipe from my great aunt Baba and is super simple. The perfect thing to have in the cookie jar for when your favorite celiac comes around.

KIT LIST
**9-inch x 5-inch x 3-inch loaf pan
stand mixer or electric hand mixer
rubber spatula (optional)
serrated bread knife
cookie sheet**

Ingredients
3 eggs
3 tablespoons superfine sugar
3 teaspoons almond extract
1 teaspoon vanilla bean paste
1¼ cups gluten-free flour
1 teaspoon baking powder
¾ cup whole almonds
unsalted butter, for greasing (use a
   dairy-free substitute if you need to)

 Store in an airtight container at room temperature for up to 5 days.

1 Preheat the oven to 400°F and line the loaf pan with parchment paper.

2 Whisk the eggs, sugar, almond extract, and vanilla paste together in a stand mixer, or in a large bowl with an electric hand mixer, until light and frothy. Sift in the flour and baking powder, then fold in. Add the almonds and fold in again.

3 Transfer to your lined pan and check that the almonds look evenly distributed throughout. If they aren't, use a little spatula or spoon to move them around in the pan. Bake for 20 minutes until light brown. Remove from the oven, then use the lining paper to lift the loaf out of the pan and let cool on a wire rack in the paper.

4 When the loaf is COMPLETELY cold, preheat the oven to 325°F and grease a cookie sheet. Peel off the lining paper and thinly slice the loaf (I used a serrated bread knife), no more than ¼ inch in thickness, then lay out the slices on the greased cookie sheet.* Depending on the size of your loaf pan, you might want to halve each slice lengthwise again to get thin fingers of biscotti perfect for dunking in tea or coffee.

5 Bake again for 25 minutes, or until golden brown, crunchy, and snappable.

✳ You might find that as you near the middle of the loaf, things are beginning to feel less like bread and more like dough, making it harder to cut. If this is the case, cut off as much as you can from either end, but leave the middle to keep cooling (it needs longer). If it still doesn't reach the right consistency (it should end up the same as the slices you already have), then just cut your losses and your loaf, and put whatever you end up with back in the oven to see what happens.

Viennese Fingers

THEY WON'T ALL MAKE IT PAST THE FINISH LINE

If you've got a food processor, this is a piece of cake (though obviously it's a cookie). If you don't have one, you can use a stand mixer, but it won't be as easy. When it comes to working with the fingers, I'd say that management of expectation is key. They're incredibly fragile, so chances are you will lose at least one. Don't worry about it; it happens to the best of us. Scoop up the crumbs with a spoon, eat them, and keep going.

KIT LIST
2 cookie sheets
food processor
pastry bag fitted with a large star tip
(Don't worry if you can't find one, as it's only for a fancy finish. You can just snip the tip off the bag instead.)

Ingredients
1½ sticks unsalted butter, softened
1¼ cups self-rising flour sifted with
   1 teaspoon baking powder
½ cup powdered sugar
3 tablespoons cornstarch
1 teaspoon vanilla bean paste or
   vanilla extract
7 ounces dark (semi-sweet) chocolate
   (54% cocoa solids minimum)

1 Preheat the oven to 350°F and line the cookie sheets with parchment paper.

2 Put all the ingredients apart from the chocolate into a food processor and blitz to a smooth paste. Transfer the mixture to the pastry bag and **pipe** onto the lined cookie sheet in sausage shapes about 3¼ inches in length. The mixture will spread considerably during baking (like literally double in size), so make sure you allow plenty of space in between.

3 Bake for 10 to 12 minutes. Remove from the oven and let cool on the cookie sheets before transferring to a wire rack. Be careful, as these are INCREDIBLY delicate!

4 Line the cookie sheets with parchment paper once again and place in the freezer for about 10 minutes (see tip on page 16). Melt the dark chocolate in a microwave-safe bowl in the microwave using the **heat, stir, repeat** method until smooth. Remove the cookie sheets from the freezer. Carefully dip the base of each Viennese finger in the chocolate, lift out using a fork to cradle it lovingly, and place, chocolate-side down, onto your ice-cold lined cookie sheets. Transfer the sheets to the fridge for a minimum of 15 minutes until the chocolate is set.

5 Once peeled off the cookie sheets, your fingers are ready to eat. They can also be enjoyed as sandwiches by whipping up a simple buttercream (see page 20), which can be piped onto the chocolate side of one Viennese finger and sandwiched together with another.

 Store in an airtight container at room temperature for up to 2 days.

Just because your fingers made it to this stage doesn't mean they're safe. If any break while you're covering them in chocolate, just use the melted chocolate as a kind of glue along the break line and hope they fuse together in the fridge.

Difficulty:

Give Me a Tuile

Inspired by the wafers I'd give away when people used to stick them in my ice cream when I was younger but that I quite like now, this recipe is simple enough, yet is all about setting up a production line to handle a multi-batch situation, with a designated spot for shaping the tuiles. There is a fair amount of mixture here as it might take a few goes to figure out the exact cooking time that will work for you (the slightest change can have a big knock-on effect), so prepare for a bit of trial and error. If you don't have heatproof hands, you'll have to find inventive ways to roll into cigar shapes.

KIT LIST

stand mixer or electric hand mixer
metal spatula (optional)
2 cookie sheets
2 silicone mats (optional)
small angled metal spatula (optional)

Ingredients

1 stick unsalted butter, softened
¾ cup powdered sugar, sifted
1 teaspoon vanilla bean paste
3 egg whites
¾ cup all-purpose flour
white chocolate, melted, and fresh
   raspberries, to serve (optional)

1 Cream the butter, powdered sugar, and vanilla paste together in a stand mixer or in a large bowl with an electric hand mixer. Gradually add the egg whites, beating constantly. Sift in the flour, then **fold** in. Cover the bowl with plastic wrap and let chill in the fridge for 30 minutes.

2 Meanwhile, preheat the oven to 400°F and line the baking sheets with parchment paper or silicone mats.

3 Take 2 tablespoons of the mixture and use the metal spatula, or a butter knife or even the back of a teaspoon, to spread it thinly and evenly onto the lining paper or mat into a rectangle with a thickness of about ¹⁄₁₆ inch. Repeat to fill the cookie sheets leaving a 2-inch gap between each rectangle to allow for spreading. You'll get about 3 rectangles per cookie sheet, so you'll have to do a few batches. Bake for 6 to 8 minutes, being sure to return any remaining mixture to the fridge in between batches.

4 Remove from the oven. You now have about 5 to 10 seconds to shape them the way you like before they harden.* If you are feeling brave, and have asbestos fingers like me, you can roll them up from one of the shorter sides and place them on a wire rack, seam-side down to stop them from unraveling. Alternatively, you can mold them around a wooden spoon handle.

5 Make sure the cookie sheets and lining paper or mats are properly cool before you start on the next batch.

6 Dip the ends in white chocolate and poke in a raspberry, if you wish, or just serve as is with your favorite ice cream.

※ If they come out of the oven with a burned border, quickly and carefully use a knife to cut these bits away, leaving a cleaner rectangle to shape. This won't give the tuile the best finish, but if you try to roll them with the burned bits, you're more likely to cause the whole thing to shatter.

Store in an airtight container at room temperature (seal as soon as you can once cooled) for up to 3 days.

Difficulty:

Pretzel Party Pieces

AND YOU'RE INVITED

These are hazelnut ganache and pretzel slices with a white chocolate and yogurt topping. Do they involve any baking? No. But they taste so good that it would have been criminal not to include this recipe. The sweetness of the ganache is offset by the saltiness of the pretzels, and the topping is a chance to get creative. I leave mine plain because I'm boring. But you're probably much more fun than me, so do what you like.

KIT LIST
9-inch square baking pan
food processor
metal spatula

Ingredients
7 ounces baked, salted pretzel snacks
3 tablespoons light corn syrup
¾ cup whole raw hazelnuts
⅔ cup heavy cream
5½ ounces milk chocolate
2¾ ounces dark (semi-sweet) chocolate
   (54% cocoa solids minimum)
7 ounces white chocolate, broken into
   small pieces
⅓ cup plain yogurt
fresh strawberries, to decorate (optional)

1 Line the baking pan with parchment paper.

2 Blitz 5½ ounces of the pretzels in a food processor until broken up but not dust, then transfer to a bowl. Add the light corn syrup and stir to combine. Press the pretzel mixture into the lined pan, using a metal spatula to flatten. Let chill in the fridge to set while you roast the hazelnuts.

3 Preheat the oven to 400°F. Spread the hazelnuts out in a small roasting pan and bake for 12 to 15 minutes until you can see the skins starting to split and blister. Remove from the oven and tip the nuts into a clean dish towel. Then wrap them up to keep the heat in and let stand for 10 minutes. This will steam the nuts and encourage the skins to come off. Massage the nuts (calm down) inside the towel (this is peeling them and doing the hard work for you). Once the majority of skins have been removed, transfer the nuts to your food processor and finely blitz.

4 Heat the cream in a small saucepan over low heat until steaming but not boiling. While the cream is heating, break up the milk and dark chocolates into small pieces and place in a heatproof bowl. Pour the hot cream over the chocolate, making sure all of it is covered, and let stand for about 5 minutes to melt before stirring vigorously to form a smooth ganache. Stir in the nuts, then pour the ganache on top of the chilled pretzel base. Return to the fridge for a minimum of an hour to set.

5 Melt the white chocolate in a microwave-safe bowl in the microwave using the **heat, stir, repeat** method, then quickly stir in the yogurt until smooth. Dip the remaining pretzels into the mixture, then arrange on top of the ganache. Alternatively, spread the mixture across the top of the ganache in a thick layer and decorate with the pretzels and fresh strawberries.

 Store in an airtight container at room temperature. They don't keep well, so eat sooner rather than later.

Difficulty: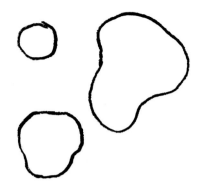

Apricot & White Chocolate Flapjack

SHUT YOUR FLAP, JACK

No, these are not pancakes. The British flapjack is a highly versatile kind of oat bar, and a bit of an all-rounder. Paired with a cup of tea? Great. Inhaled as a snack on the go? Convenient. Carved into a slice for breakfast? Cheeky but acceptable. A good recipe to make with kids, these can be put together with any type of dried fruit.

KIT LIST
9-inch square baking pan

Ingredients
1 stick unsalted butter
3 tablespoons light corn syrup
2 tablespoons condensed milk
2 cups rolled oats
¾ cup chopped ready-to-eat dried apricots
½ teaspoon fine salt
3½ ounces white chocolate, chopped

1 Preheat the oven to 400°F and line the baking pan with parchment paper.

2 Melt the butter with the light corn syrup and condensed milk in a large saucepan over low heat, then remove from the heat and stir in the oats, apricots, and salt. Let the mixture cool a little before stirring in the white chocolate, otherwise it will melt immediately and you want some lumps intact when it goes into the oven.

3 Transfer the mixture to the lined pan and spread evenly. Bake for 20 minutes, or until just starting to turn golden on top. Remove from the oven and let cool completely in the pan.

4 Use the lining paper to lift the flapjack out of the pan and slice into squares.

 Store in an airtight container at room temperature for up to 4 days.

Three-Cheese Crisps

THIS MIGHT NOT EVEN QUALIFY AS A RECIPE

This is so simple that I'm embarrassed to write it down and call it a recipe. It's literally just cheese turned crisp, but they are great snacks for parties. Or for people who like cheese.

KIT LIST
cookie sheet
2-inch round cookie cutter

Ingredients
½ cup grated sharp cheddar cheese
¼ cup grated Parmesan cheese
¼ cup grated Gouda cheese
freshly ground black pepper

1 Preheat the oven to 425°F and line a baking sheet with parchment paper.

2 Add the grated cheeses to a large bowl and add a liberal amount of black pepper. Use your fingertips to mix (a spoon will cause the cheese to stick together in a ball).

3 Place the cookie cutter on the lined cookie sheet and add 2 tablespoons of the grated cheese mixture to the inside of the cutter, then remove the cutter, leaving you with a circle of cheese. Use your fingers to gently fill any gaps or spread more evenly. Continue until you have used up all the cheese, leaving a gap in between each circle to allow for spreading during baking.

4 Bake for 6 to 8 minutes, depending on how crisp you want them. Remove from the oven and let cool slightly on the baking sheet.* Be careful because they're very hot!

* If you haven't spaced the crisps out enough, they might all have merged into a big cheese rectangle. You can either just eat this (no judgment) or use a knife or cookie cutter to carefully create the shape you were hoping for. But do this before the crisp has cooled or they will crack.

Store in an airtight container at room temperature for up to 3 days.

HMM...

Cakes are Boring

I take it back, cakes aren't boring—they're my favorite. And if you're anything like me, the minute you get a new recipe book, the cake section is the first bit you turn to. Cake is what it's all about.

There are quite a few really rich, indulgent cakes in this chapter for when you need a treat, such as the Toffee Apple Crumble Cake on pages 72–5. But I've also gone for a lot of fruit-based bakes (doing my bit to make sure you get your five-a-day), so there are some lighter, cleaner flavors for when you need something a bit more refreshing (for example, Is It a Key Lime Pie? on pages 50–1).

Some of these are bakes I've been making for friends and family for years, while others are crazy new ideas I had for the book. Really hoping you won't be able to tell the difference.

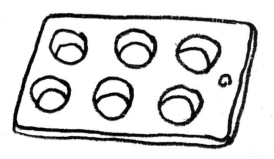

Is It a Key Lime Pie?

PLOT TWIST ... IT'S A CAKE

This is basically the cake version of a key lime pie. I stole the idea from a child. Sorry Sienna.

KIT LIST
food processor
2 8-inch round cake pans (ideally
    loose-bottomed)
stand mixer or electric hand mixer
Microplane
spatula (optional)
toothpick
metal spatula
cake board (optional)

Ingredients
3 sticks unsalted butter, softened,
    plus extra for greasing
1⅓ cups superfine sugar, plus
    1 to 2 tablespoons for the syrup
4 eggs
6 large limes
2¾ cups all-purpose flour, sifted with
    1 tablespoon baking powder
1½ cups coarse cookie crumbs (I blitz
    Biscoff speculoos cookies in a food
    processor but you could also use
    graham wafers or your favorite cookies.)

For the buttercream
2¼ sticks unsalted butter, softened
2½ cups powdered sugar
1 tablespoon vanilla bean paste
green gel coloring (optional)

**Store in an airtight container
in a cool place (not the fridge)
for up to 3 days.**

1 Preheat the oven to 400°F. Grease your cake pans and line the bases with parchment paper.

2 Cream the butter and sugar together in a stand mixer, or in a large bowl with an electric hand mixer, for 3 minutes. Add the eggs one at a time, beating well after each. Use a Microplane to **zest** 2 of the limes and add to the mixture. **Fold** in the prepared flour, being sure not to mix too vigorously or the cake will become dense. Divide between the prepared pans and bake for 20 to 25 minutes until golden brown and the cakes spring back when pressed with a precarious finger.

3 Meanwhile, to make the lime syrup, halve all 6 limes and squeeze the juice into a small saucepan. Add 1 tablespoon superfine sugar. Place over medium heat and bring to a boil, then reduce the heat and simmer for 3 minutes. Use a teaspoon to take a little of the syrup, wait for it to cool, and taste it. It should be zingy and sour. If you want it sweeter, add another tablespoon of superfine sugar, return to the boil and, once the sugar has dissolved, simmer for another 3 minutes. Remove from the heat and set aside.

4 Remove the cakes from the oven. Use a toothpick to make little holes all over the top of both cakes, then pour the syrup evenly over them. Let cool completely in the pans.

5 While the cakes are cooling, make the buttercream. Beat the butter in your stand mixer or in a large bowl with your electric hand mixer until smooth. Sift in the powdered sugar and add the vanilla paste, along with a little green gel coloring if you wish. Beat again.*

6 Remove the cakes from their pans and peel off the paper. Set one cake, bottom-side up, on a serving plate or cake board (use a little of the buttercream between the cake and plate or board to secure it if necessary). Spread buttercream on the top of the cake with a metal spatula and scatter with half the cookie crumbs. Stack the second cake on top, again bottom-side up, spread with the remaining buttercream, and scatter with the cookie crumbs.

✳ Is your buttercream lumpy? Then your butter's too cold. If you're willing to live life on the edge, put the buttercream in the microwave for no longer than 15 seconds and then beat vigorously.

Difficulty:

Strawberry Shortcake Roll(er Coaster)

FOR LIFE'S UPS & DOWNS

This tastes like a cheesecake in a jelly roll. There is a chance you'll end up with parchment paper inside as an unwanted, extra ingredient. But you've got to take the rough with the smooth.

KIT LIST
**Jelly roll pan or flat-bottomed baking pan, about 9¹/₂ inches x 13¹/₂ inches
stand mixer or electric hand mixer
rubber spatula**

Ingredients
unsalted butter, for greasing
4 large eggs
⅓ cup superfine sugar
¾ cup all-purpose flour, sifted with
    1 teaspoon baking powder
1 cup cream cheese
⅓ cup powdered sugar
1 tablespoon vanilla bean paste
1¾ cups chopped fresh strawberries
¾ cup cookie crumbs of your choice
    (I use digestive biscuits but you could
    also use graham wafers.)
1¾ ounces white chocolate, broken
    into pieces

1 Preheat the oven to 350°F. Grease the baking pan and line with parchment paper.

2 Beat the eggs and superfine sugar together in a stand mixer or in a large bowl with an electric hand mixer until they reach the **ribbon stage**. Gently **fold** in the prepared flour with a spatula and pour into the lined pan. Bake for 15 minutes until golden brown.

3 While the cake is baking, add the cream cheese to the bowl of your stand mixer or a large bowl, sift in the powdered sugar, and add the vanilla paste. Then whisk with your mixer or your electric hand mixer just until combined.* Stir in half the strawberries. Cover the bowl with plastic wrap and refrigerate until ready to use.

4 Line a cutting board with parchment paper. Remove the cake from the oven and invert onto the lined board. Peel off the top lining paper, then roll up the cake from one of the shorter sides, making sure to roll up the new paper with it. If it looks like it's going to unfurl, wedge a heavy item either side of the rolled cake to keep it intact. Let cool completely.

5 Gently unroll and spread the cream cheese mixture across the cake. Top with some of the remaining strawberries and half of the cookie crumbs, then reroll, this time leaving the paper out. Melt the white chocolate in a microwave-safe bowl in the microwave using the **heat, stir, repeat** method until you can drizzle it over the cake, then scatter with the remaining strawberries and cookie crumbs to serve.

 Store in an airtight container in the fridge for up to 2 days.

✳ Be careful not to overdo it because if you overwhisk it, it will become too runny to use later on. If you're worried about this happening, you could do it using a hand whisk. If you do end up with a liquid, you'll just have to go out to the store for more cream cheese.

Difficulty:

Eton Mess Gateaux

THIS CAKE IS TRYING ITS BEST TO IMPRESS YOU

This is a sexy cake. As well as being delicious with all the fresh flavors of an Eton Mess, it's also not bad to look at, so a good bake to whip out for summer parties or to use as a centerpiece.

KIT LIST
food processor
2 8-inch round cake pans
stand mixer or electric hand mixer
2 cookie sheets
2 or 3 pastry bags
star tip (optional)
rubber spatula
small paintbrush (optional)
cake board (optional)

For the puree
3 cups fresh strawberries
1½ cups fresh raspberries

For the cakes
2 sticks unsalted butter, plus extra
    for greasing
1 cup superfine sugar
3 eggs
2 cups all-purpose flour, sifted with
    2 teaspoons baking powder

For the meringues
3 egg whites
pinch of salt
¾ cup superfine sugar
red or pink gel food coloring (optional)

For the filling and topping
2 cups heavy cream
1 tablespoon vanilla bean paste
1⅓ cups fresh hulled and sliced
    strawberries, plus extra to decorate

To make the puree

1 Hull and coarsely chop the strawberries. Place in a food processor with the raspberries. Blitz until no big lumps remain.

2 Pour this puree into a medium saucepan and place over low heat. Normally I would put a splash of water in, but the purpose of this step is to remove the water to make a thick, reduced puree. Let the mixture bubble away until **reduced** by half, then remove from the heat and let cool. Half of this will be used in the cake batter and half will be spread onto the baked cakes.

To make the cake layers

3 Preheat the oven to 400°F. Grease the cake pans and line with parchment paper.

4 **Cream** the butter and sugar together in a stand mixer or in a large bowl with an electric hand mixer for a minimum of 5 minutes. Add the eggs one at a time, beating well after each addition. Sift in the prepared flour and pour half of the puree on top. Gently **fold** in to combine. Divide the mixture evenly between the lined pans and bake for about 20 minutes, or until golden.

5 Let the cakes cool slightly in the pans, then remove from the pans and transfer to a wire rack to cool completely.

The fruit puree is well worth doing. I once made this cake without it and the result was a very stodgy cake that didn't taste at all of strawberry or raspberry.

To make the meringues

6 Reduce or preheat the oven to 300°F. Place one of your cake pans on top of a piece of parchment paper and draw around it with a pencil, then use the paper to line one cookie sheet.

7 Whisk the egg whites in your stand mixer or in a large bowl with your electric hand mixer (all kit thoroughly cleaned before reusing) until **soft peaks** start to form.

8 Add the salt and then the sugar, 1 tablespoon at a time every 30 seconds, whisking constantly. Once the sugar is all incorporated, whisk for another 3 minutes. Test the meringue is done by rubbing a little of the mixture between your thumb and forefinger. If you CANNOT feel any grains of sugar, it's ready.

9 Roll down a pastry bag and fill with some of the meringue mixture using a spatula. **Pipe** onto the circle marked on the lining paper, starting at the center of the circle and working outward. Bake for an hour.

10 Meanwhile, line your second cookie sheet with parchment paper. Take a clean pastry bag (fitted with the star tip, if using). If using coloring, paint a little gel in 2 or 3 stripes on the inside of the pastry bag from the tip to the top. Fill with meringue mixture and pipe little meringue kisses on the lined tray. (If not using the star tip, just snip the end off the bag before piping.) Don't worry about crowding the sheet, as meringues don't spread the way cookies do, but make sure none of them are touching. The color, if using, may take some time to come out, so do a few practice ones to get the rhythm of it all.

11 Bake the meringue kisses for 45 minutes. When the cooking time is up, turn off the heat, open the oven door, and let the meringues cool down slowly inside the oven.

To assemble

12 Use your stand mixer or electric hand mixer again to whisk the cream and vanilla paste to **soft peaks**, then transfer to another clean pastry bag (fitted with a star tip, if you wish). It might seem like the cream is too soft or runny to be suitable for piping, but don't worry, it will stiffen as you work it in the bag.

13 Peel the lining paper from the cakes and place one, bottom-side up, on your cake board or plate. Spread half of the remaining puree on top of the cake, then scatter it with some of the sliced strawberries and pipe some cream splodges on top.* Stack the meringue circle on top and spread with more cream, followed by some more sliced strawberries. Stack the other cake on top, again bottom-side up. Spread the top with the last of the puree, then decorate with your meringue kisses and any remaining strawberries.

✳ If you start piping the cream and find there is no definition to your splodges, pipe some practice ones elsewhere until it reaches the right consistency.

 Store in an airtight container in the fridge, though this needs to be eaten as soon as possible, so get involved.

SEE JUST HOW SEXY THIS CAKE IS... ➔ ➔

Jaffa Orange Brownies

THE BROWNIE THAT WILL END THE CAKE VS COOKIE DEBATE

Making your own jaffa jelly means you can be totally in control of how sour or sweet it is. But no judgment if you use store-bought jelly instead. To be honest, if I wasn't writing a recipe book, that's what I'd do.

KIT LIST
Microplane
hand whisk
2 12-inch x 9-inch baking pans
stand mixer or electric hand mixer
rubber spatula (optional)
round cookie cutter, about 1¼-inch
pastry bag (optional)
baking pan

For the jelly topping
4 sheets of gelatin, about ¾ ounce in total
zest of 2 oranges, plus extra to decorate
1¾ cups freshly squeezed orange juice, strained of seeds and pith
1 tablespoon gelling sugar
1 tablespoon Cointreau (optional)

To make the jelly topping

1 To make the jelly topping, **bloom** the gelatin in a small amount of cold water. Meanwhile, put the orange zest and juice and jam sugar into a saucepan and boil until the sugar has dissolved. Remove from the heat and add the Cointreau, if using. Squeeze the water out of the gelatin and add it to the juice mixture, then whisk with a hand whisk until dissolved. Line one of the baking pans with plastic wrap and pour the jelly in. Let cool to room temperature, then place in the fridge for a couple of hours to set.

To make the brownies

2 Preheat the oven to 375°F and line the second baking pan with parchment paper. Melt the dark chocolate and butter in a saucepan over low heat, stirring until smooth. Put both the sugars into the bowl of a stand mixer or a large bowl and add the chocolate mixture, whisking on a fast speed with the mixer or an electric hand mixer. Continue whisking for about 3 minutes until the mixture is lukewarm. Add the eggs one at a time, beating well after each addition. Carefully **fold** in the flour, then transfer the mixture to the lined pan. Bake for 15 to 18 minutes until slightly crispy on top but with a slight wobble. Remove from the oven and let cool completely in the pan.

3 Once cool, invert the pan onto a cutting board and peel off the paper. Trim the edges to make clean sides and then slice into squares. I like a larger brownie (shock), so I make 12 from this, but you can make them bite-sized by slicing into smaller squares.

WAIT, THERE'S MORE...

For the brownies

11½ ounces dark (semi-sweet) chocolate (54% cocoa solids minimum), broken into pieces

1 stick unsalted butter

½ cup superfine sugar

½ cup lightly packed soft light brown sugar

3 eggs

1 cup all-purpose flour

10½ ounces milk chocolate, broken into pieces

To assemble

4 This next bit is not an easy maneuver. You want to lift the jelly out of the pan using the plastic wrap, then flip it over onto a cutting board and peel off the plastic wrap. Then use a suitably sized cookie cutter to stamp out circles of jelly and set one on top of each brownie square. Transfer to the fridge to keep cold.

5 Melt the milk chocolate in a microwave-safe bowl in the microwave using the **heat, stir, repeat** method until smooth. Place the brownies on a wire rack over a baking pan and spoon the melted chocolate over the top. The aim is to use the chocolate to lock down the jelly, so you need to cover the whole top—you don't want to see even a glimpse of orange. The chocolate might drip down the sides, but as long as the jelly remains covered, you're safe.* If you are after a neater finish, you can **pipe** the chocolate on instead.

6 Chill in the fridge until ready to serve, but remember to remove 15 minutes beforehand to allow them to reach room temperature. Top with a little orange zest for a jazzy finish.

＊If, despite your best efforts, the circle of jelly slithers down the side of your brownie square, you have two options:
1) scrape it off and you've got yourself a pretty boring but tasty chocolate brownie;
2) remake the jelly in a wider baking pan so that your circles of jelly don't end up as thick and heavy.

 Store in an airtight container in the fridge for up to 2 days.

Difficulty:

Take-Me-Back Traybake

BACK TO SCHOOL THAT IS—THIS ISN'T FOR YOUR EX

The traybake of your childhood dreams or nightmares, depending on what the food was like in your school cafeteria. I did some very scientific Instagram market research for this, and heard rumors of a pink custard, so I think there are lots of variations. This recipe is based on what I remember—cake with raspberries and coconut—but put whatever you want on there for your own throwback; chocolate and sprinkles, for example.

KIT LIST
13-inch x 9-inch cake pan
stand mixer or electric hand mixer
hand whisk
rubber spatula (optional)
metal spatula
cake board (optional)

Ingredients
2½ sticks unsalted butter, softened
1¼ cups superfine sugar
5 eggs
1 tablespoon vanilla bean paste
2½ cups all-purpose flour sifted with
    2 teaspoons baking powder
¼ cup raspberry jam, at room temperature,
    plus 3 tablespoons for the topping
½ cup fresh raspberries
½ cup desiccated coconut
custard, to serve (see page 183 for
    homemade)

 Store in an airtight container at room temperature for up to 4 days.

1 Preheat the oven to 375°F and line the baking pan with parchment paper.

2 **Cream** the butter and the sugar together in a stand mixer or in a large bowl with an electric hand mixer for 5 minutes. In a separate bowl, whisk the eggs and vanilla paste together with a hand whisk until well mixed, then gradually add to the creamed mixture, a little at a time, whisking constantly until combined.

3 Sift in the prepared flour and gently **fold** in to combine. Transfer half of the cake batter to the lined pan and spread evenly with a metal spatula. Drop the ¼ cup of jam, 1 tablespoon at a time, on top and spread. If the jam is not spreading, it is too cold, so just pop it in the microwave for a few seconds to loosen it if needed. Once the jam is spread, break up the raspberries and scatter them over the jam. Top with the remaining cake batter and spread evenly.* Bake for 25 minutes, or until golden brown.

4 Remove from the oven and let cool completely in the pan. Invert onto a cake board or serving plate and peel off the lining paper. Heat the remaining 3 tablespoons of jam in the microwave or in a small saucepan on the burner and spread evenly over the top of the cake. Scatter with the coconut and serve with warm custard for a true hit of school cafeteria nostalgia.

* If you get to this stage and realize you used too much of your batter on the bottom half and your top layer is too thin, then you might find the odd bit of raspberry or jam poking through. Scrape whatever batter you can from your bowl to cover up these spots, just like plastering holes in a wall, which I do ALL THE TIME.

Difficulty:

S'more Cupcakes

GIMME, GIMME S'MORE

This recipe is for a chocolate cupcake with a biscuit base, a core of rich ganache, and a toasty marshmallow top. The cupcake bit is easy, the marshmallow bit is hard. And sticky. But if you get through it, you'll have made your own marshmallow, which is a really useful, transferable life skill. You could use it as cement or to stick posters to your wall or something.

KIT LIST
12-hole muffin pan
12 large cupcake baking cups
2½-inch round cookie cutter
stand mixer or electric hand mixer
rubber spatula (optional)
2 pastry bags
sugar thermometer
¾-inch round cookie cutter (optional)

For the cupcakes
2¼ ounces dark (semi-sweet) chocolate (54% cocoa solids minimum), chopped
12 digestive biscuits, plus extras to allow for breakages (you can use graham wafers)
1¼ sticks unsalted butter, softened
⅔ cup firmly packed soft light brown sugar
3 eggs
1 tablespoon freshly brewed coffee, cooled
1 cup all-purpose flour sifted with 1 teaspoon baking powder
1 tablespoon unsweetened cocoa powder

For the ganache
½ cup heavy cream
5½ ounces milk chocolate

For the marshmallow
⅔ cup superfine sugar
½ cup, plus 1 tablespoon, cold water
⅓ cup liquid glucose
3 sheets of gelatin, about ½ ounce

1 Preheat the oven to 375°F and line the muffin pan with the baking cups.

2 Melt the dark chocolate in a microwave-safe bowl in the microwave using the **heat, stir, repeat** method until smooth. Leave to cool while you carry out the next couple of steps.

3 Using the larger cookie cutter, press out a circle from each of the digestive biscuits (or graham wafers) and set one into the bottom of each cup.

4 **Cream** the butter and sugar together in a stand mixer or in a large bowl with an electric hand mixer. Add the eggs one at a time, beating well after each addition.

5 Pour in the cooled melted chocolate and cold coffee and beat again. Sift in the prepared flour and cocoa powder, then **fold** in to combine. Divide the batter evenly between the 12 baking cups, then bake for 18 minutes. Remove from the oven and let cool completely in the muffin pan.

6 To make the ganache, heat the cream in a small saucepan over low heat until steaming but not boiling. While the cream is heating, break up the chocolate into small pieces and place in a heatproof bowl. Pour the hot cream over the chocolate, making sure all of it is covered, and let stand for about 5 minutes to melt before stirring vigorously to form a smooth ganache. Let cool for about 10 minutes before transferring to a pastry bag. Set aside while you make the marshmallow.

7 This next bit should happen all at once, so recruit some extra hands if you can. To make the marshmallow, put the sugar, ¼ cup of cold water, and 2 tablespoons of the liquid glucose into a small saucepan over medium heat. Put the gelatin with

¼ cup plus 1 teaspoon cold water in another small saucepan and place over low heat until melted. Put the remaining liquid glucose in a microwave-safe bowl and microwave for 30 seconds, then pour into the bowl of the stand mixer or a large bowl and whisk on a slow speed with the mixer or the electric hand mixer. When the sugar mixture on the burner reaches 240°F on a sugar thermometer, remove from the heat and gradually pour down the side of the bowl. Then pour in the melted gelatin. Mix on a fast speed for 8 minutes. Transfer to a pastry bag* and set aside.

8 Using the small cookie cutter, cut out the central core of each cooled cupcake (or you could gently press a water bottle top into the cake as a rough guide and use a knife). Save the crumbs for cake pops (see page 64). Preheat your broiler to medium.

9 Fill each hole with ganache up to the top of the cupcake. **Pipe** marshmallow on the top of the cupcake, ensuring no cake is showing. Put 2 cupcakes under the broiler at a time and DO NOT WALK AWAY. This step takes seconds as you just want the marshmallow to toast slightly. Remove from the broiler and eat straightaway for an oozy chocolate middle, or let cool if you prefer a firmer center.

 Store in an airtight container at room temperature for up to 3 days. And before serving, try popping them in the microwave quickly before eating to give you a gooey center.

✳ You might not encounter any difficulties at all here. Or, filling a plastic bag with the stickiest substance on earth might throw up some challenges. Remind yourself of the best way to fill a pastry bag by checking the glossary on page 10. Then, if you find that the marshmallow is sticking at the top of the bag and refusing to move down, hold the bag very, very tightly together just above the filling and swing it up and down and around and around, as if drawing a big circle by your side. The idea is to get a downward swing that will force the marshmallow to the tip of the bag. Be careful not to hit anyone or anything.

Cake Pops

THESE COULD ALSO BE CALLED TRUFFLES IF I WASN'T
TRYING TO MAKE THEM FIT INTO THE CAKE CHAPTER

In the spirit of waste not, want not, I started making these to use up leftover cake crumbs and chocolate buttercream. I've adapted it here to use ganache because it's slightly less sweet. If you have leftover anything from this book, just roll it into a ball and cover it with chocolate. Maybe not the pork pies.

KIT LIST
cookie sheet
sugar thermometer (if tempering)

Ingredients
½ cup heavy cream
5½ ounces milk chocolate
1 cup leftover cake crumbs (if you have less
   or more crumbs, then adjust the other
   ingredient amounts accordingly)
3 tablespoons cream cheese
14 ounces white chocolate, broken into
   pieces

1 Starting with the ganache, heat the cream in a small saucepan over low heat until steaming but not boiling. While the cream is heating, break up the milk chocolate into small pieces and place in a heatproof bowl. Pour the hot cream over the chocolate, making sure all of it is covered. Let stand to melt for about 5 minutes before stirring vigorously to form a smooth ganache. Let cool for about 10 minutes. Meanwhile, line the cookie sheet with parchment paper.

2 Place the cake crumbs in a large bowl. Mix in the cooled ganache and be rough with it, until the crumbs break down evenly and are coated in the ganache. You may not need all of the chocolate, or you may need a bit more depending on the consistency of your crumbs. Stir in the cream cheese. Roll into little balls (or big balls, depending on how you like your cake pops), ensuring a smooth, not cracked, consistency. Place on the lined cookie sheet and chill in the fridge for an hour to harden up.

3 Start **tempering** the white chocolate shortly before your cake balls are due out of the fridge. Place 10½ ounces of the chocolate in a heatproof bowl set over a pan of simmering water* (do not let the bowl touch the water) until it reaches 113°F on a sugar thermometer (this will happen quicker than you think). Then add the reserved chocolate in 4 goes, stirring vigorously after each addition until fully melted. By the end of this process, you're looking for the chocolate to have reached about 86°F and be fully incorporated.

4 At this point, the chocolate will set hard and fast, so you need to move quickly. Lower your cake balls into the chocolate, then use a fork to lift out (wiggling off any excess) and place back on your lined cookie sheet. If you've tempered the chocolate correctly, they will set when the chocolate cools and then crack when you bite into them.**

✳ The eagle-eyed among you will notice that you have just created a **bain-marie**. (Proof that it was worth me writing that glossary on pages 9–11.) This method allows you to closely monitor the temperature of the chocolate as it melts, something you wouldn't be able to do if using the **heat, stir, repeat** method.

** If the chocolate isn't setting, you haven't tempered it quite right (this time). Just put the chocolate-covered balls in the fridge (or freezer if you're against the clock). They'll still taste good, but they'll be missing that pleasing crack when you bite into them.

If you've successfully tempered the chocolate, store in an airtight container somewhere cool for up to 3 days. If you haven't, put them in the fridge.

Orange & Passion Fruit "Mousse" Cake Jars

IT'S A MOUTHFUL

I've called this a cake but it might be more of a trifle. Whatever it is, it's delicious and fairly easy to make. The recipe uses a jaconde sponge cake, so you can impress people with that. What they don't need to know is that the mousse is a bit of a cheat. This is very sweet, which is why I use the bitters dashed on top. And serve it in whatever you want (old jam jars, bourbon glasses, etc).

KIT LIST
2 jelly roll pans or flat-bottomed baking pans, 9¹/₂ inches x 13¹/₂ inches
food processor
Microplane
stand mixer or electric hand mixer
rubber spatula (optional)
small metal spatula
large pastry bag
cookie cutter the same diameter as the jars or glasses
jars or glasses, to serve

*To make the most out of your pulp, blitz it in a food processor before you strain it.

1 Preheat the oven to 425°F and line the baking pans with parchment paper.

2 To make the sponge cakes, first blitz the ground almonds, powdered sugar, and flour together in a food processor. This makes the mixture super fine. Add the orange zest and whole eggs and blitz again to make a paste.

3 Whisk the egg whites in a stand mixer or in a large bowl with an electric hand mixer until white and foamy. Add the superfine sugar 1 tablespoon at a time, whisking constantly. When the final sugar has been added, continue to whisk for another couple of minutes. Rub some of the mixture between your thumb and forefinger, it should feel smooth, not grainy (sticky too, obvs.). If it is still grainy, continue to whisk until the sugar has dissolved.

4 Stir one-third of the egg whites into the almond batter until combined, then gently **fold** in the rest of the whites. Fold in the melted butter, then transfer the batter to the lined pans, spread out evenly with a small metal spatula, and bake for about 10 to 12 minutes until golden brown. Remove the sponge cakes from the oven and let cool completely in the pans (they are supposed to be very flat, so don't panic).

5 While the sponge cakes are cooling, make the mousse. Halve 6 passion fruit, scoop out the pulp, and push through a strainer into a bowl.* Discard the seeds. Add the lemon juice and the condensed milk and stir to combine. In a separate bowl, whip the cream to **soft peaks** and fold this into the passion-fruit mixture, then transfer to a large pastry bag. Put this in the fridge while you return your attention to the sponge cakes.

WAIT, THERE'S MORE...

For the jaconde sponge cakes

1⅓ cups ground almonds
2 cups powdered sugar
⅔ cups all-purpose flour
zest of 1 orange
5 eggs, plus 4 egg whites
¼ cup superfine sugar
3 tablespoons unsalted butter, melted
a few dashes of Angostura bitters

For the mousse

8 to 10 fresh passion fruit, depending
   on size
juice of ½ lemon
1 cup condensed milk
1¼ cups heavy cream

6 Using the cookie cutter, stamp out circles of sponge cake from the pans and set aside. I aim to have 2 circles of sponge cake in each jar. Halve the remaining passion fruit and scoop the pulp into a small bowl.

7 Now to assemble. Take a jar and squish a circle of sponge cake into the bottom of it. Drizzle it with a little dash of bitters and let it soak in before topping with a bit of passion-fruit pulp. Then **pipe** on a circle of mousse to cover. Stack with a second circle of sponge cake and repeat the process. Finish each jar with a little dollop of passion-fruit pulp and serve.

 Store in an airtight container in the fridge for up to 2 days.

Difficulty:

Mango & Grapefruit Crème Brûlée Cheesecake

CRUSH, WHIP & SPREAD IT. NO, REALLY.

To me, cheesecake is always too sweet and that's why I wanted to give this a sour kick. The grapefruit is a little bit different and creates a surprise in the middle. Originally, the crème brûlée topping required a blowtorch, but I have since had an unfortunate incident where I set fire to one in my hands (in front of a room full of people), so I've practiced the broiler method instead. Much safer, but less likely to give you a good story. And just a heads-up, this tastes best if you let it set overnight.

KIT LIST
9-inch round, loose-bottomed cake pan, at least 3½ inches deep
food processor (optional)
stand mixer or electric hand mixer
rubber spatula (optional)
metal spatula

Ingredients
1¼ cups chopped fresh mango flesh (chop the pieces into ½-inch cubes)
juice of 1 pink grapefruit
3 teaspoons vanilla bean paste
9 ounces gingersnaps (you could make your own—see page 29)
1 stick unsalted butter, melted
3½ cups cream cheese (I use Philadelphia)
1 cup superfine sugar, plus ¼ cup for topping
3 eggs
¾ cup plain yogurt
¼ cup all-purpose flour

1 Preheat the oven to 400°F. Line the bottom and up the insides of the cake pan with parchment paper.

2 Put the mango and grapefruit juice into a large saucepan over low heat, cover with a lid, and heat until gently simmering for about 10 minutes. When the mango starts to break down to a pulp, stir in 1 teaspoon of the vanilla paste and let cool.

3 Meanwhile, blitz the gingersnaps in a food processor until you have crumbs, or seal them in a ziplock bag and smash them with a rolling pin to get the same result. Add the melted butter and stir together, then press into your lined pan using the back of the spoon to get a smooth finish. Bake for 5 minutes, then remove from the oven and let cool (but leave the oven on).

4 Beat the cream cheese in a stand mixer or in a large bowl with an electric hand mixer until smooth. This will take a matter of seconds, so do not overbeat it. Add the sugar and beat again until just incorporated. In a separate bowl, beat the eggs and remaining 2 teaspoons vanilla paste together, then beat in the yogurt. Gradually add the egg mixture to the cream cheese mixture, beating constantly. Lastly, sift in the flour and then **fold** in using a spatula or spoon. You should have a smooth creamy mixture at this point, so make sure it is well mixed.

WAIT, THERE'S MORE... ➤

5 Pour half of the cheesecake mixture onto the cooled crust and spread out using a metal spatula. Using a teaspoon, dollop the mango mixture all over the top as evenly as you can. Pour the remaining cheesecake mixture on top of this and spread it out. Be gentle here or you'll disturb the mango underneath.

6 Bear with me for this bit: it's for giving you a cheesecake that doesn't have a crack down the middle and this is achieved by taking things slowly. Bake for 10 minutes, then reduce the heat to 225°F and bake for another 30 minutes. Turn the oven off but leave the cheesecake in for another 30 minutes, then open the door and leave it for another 30 minutes. It should now be cool enough to put in the fridge for 4 hours, or ideally overnight.

7 For the topping, sprinkle the cheesecake with the remaining sugar and use the back of a spoon to press it down so that it is tightly packed. Put the whole thing in the freezer for 30 minutes. (You are not looking to completely freeze the cheesecake at this point, just to set the topping in place and prevent everything from melting during the next step.)

8 Preheat your broiler to medium–high. Pop your cheesecake out of the pan, removing the parchment paper from the sides only, and place it under the broiler. Stand in front of it and watch it like nothing else matters (shout out to Metallica). The sugar will start to caramelize, brown, and melt together to make a solid sugar topping, just like a crème brûlée.* This will take a matter of minutes, no longer, or you'll do funny things to the cheesecake. Remove from the broiler and wait for it to come back to room temperature before putting it back in the fridge for an hour before FINALLY serving. It sounds like a faff but it is totally worth it.

***** If you aren't getting a bubbly, brown top, remove the cheesecake from the broiler and use a spoon to make the sugar even more compact on the top. Put it back under the broiler and crank up the heat. It's better to have this under a really hot broiler for a brief amount of time than to keep it slowly cooking under lower heat.

 Store in the fridge. This won't last long once the top has been broiled, so try to eat it the same day.

Difficulty:

Toffee Apple Crumble Cake

THIS CAKE IS TOO HEAVY TO EAT ON A STICK. I'VE TRIED.

This cake tastes pretty great. It's a combination of an apple crumble and a cake, with a pretty serious cream situation going on in the middle. I love this recipe, but I can't lie to you. It's not easy. It's the kind of thing you should do when you really want someone to know you've made an effort. A good cake for anyone who doesn't like things too sweet, you can tart up the flavor and even throw in some booze if you feel so inclined. Good luck.

KIT LIST
2 8-inch round cake pans
stand mixer or electric hand mixer
rubber spatula (optional)
food processor
hand whisk
baking pan
2 pastry bags
cake board (optional)

For the cake layers
1¼ sticks unsalted butter, softened, plus extra for greasing
½ cup superfine sugar
3 eggs
1 cup all-purpose flour sifted with 1 teaspoon baking powder
½ teaspoon ground ginger
¼ teaspoon ground cinnamon
pinch of salt
2 baking apples, peeled, cored, and chopped into about ½-inch pieces

For the crumble topping
¼ cup soft light brown sugar
¼ cup turbinado sugar
½ teaspoon ground cinnamon
½ teaspoon salt
¾ stick unsalted butter, chilled and cubed
¾ cup all-purpose flour
¼ cup rolled oats

For the sour apple puree
1 baking apple, peeled, cored, and coarsely chopped
1 teaspoon superfine sugar
2 tablespoons water
juice of 1 lemon
2 tablespoons unsalted butter
1 teaspoon vanilla bean paste
splash of Calvados (optional)

For the crème pâtissière
3 sheets of gelatin, about ½ ounce
2 egg yolks
¼ cup superfine sugar
1 tablespoon cornstarch
1 cup milk
⅔ cup heavy cream
1 tablespoon vanilla bean extract

For the caramel drizzle
¾ stick unsalted butter
⅔ cup firmly packed soft light brown sugar
1 tablespoon water
3½ tablespoons evaporated milk

 Store in an airtight container in a cold place (not the fridge) for up to 3 days.

To make the cake layers and crumble topping

1 Preheat the oven to 400°F. Grease the cake pans and line with parchment paper.

2 To make the cakes, **cream** the butter and sugar together in a stand mixer or in a large bowl with an electric hand mixer. Add the eggs one at a time, beating well after each. Sift in the prepared flour and spices, add the salt and apple, and **fold** into the batter. Divide evenly between the lined pans and set aside.

3 To make the crumble topping, put all the ingredients into a food processor and pulse until the mixture looks like breadcrumbs. Divide between the pans to cover the cake batter. (I use my hands to sprinkle it evenly.) Bake for 25 to 30 minutes until the crumble topping is golden brown. Remove from the oven and let cool completely in the pans. While the cakes are baking and cooling, make the other elements.

To make the sour apple puree

4 Put the apple, sugar, measured water, and lemon juice into a medium saucepan over medium heat and stir occasionally, mashing up the apple as it begins to soften. Remove from the heat, stir in the butter, vanilla paste, and Calvados (if using) and let cool.

To make the crème pâtissière

5 Put the sheets of gelatin into a small bowl of cold water and set aside for 10 minutes to **bloom**.

6 Whisk the egg yolks, sugar, and cornstarch together in a bowl with a hand whisk until you have a pale paste. Heat the milk and cream in a medium saucepan over low heat, stirring, until steaming but not boiling. Add the vanilla extract and stir to combine. Pour a little of the hot milk mixture onto the egg yolk mixture and whisk vigorously to combine. Add the egg yolk mixture to the pan, increase the heat gradually, and stir constantly until the mixture thickens and starts to boil (it should coat the back of a spoon and when a line is drawn with your finger on the spoon it should stay visible). Boil for 2 minutes to **cook out** the cornstarch, continuing to stir. Squeeze any excess

✳ If your cooled crème pâtissière is lumpy, you should push it through a strainer before you put it in the pastry bag. Use a spoon to work through any lumps and bumps so that you have a much smoother custard coming out the other side.

water from the gelatin, then add to the pan and whisk in. Transfer to a baking pan and spread out evenly to cool, covering with plastic wrap that is loose enough for you to press it down across the entire surface of the custard to stop a skin from forming. Once cool, transfer to a pastry bag.*

To make the caramel drizzle

7 Heat the butter, sugar, and measured water in a small saucepan and stir until the sugar dissolves. Boil for a couple of minutes until it starts to darken to a golden brown, then pour in the evaporated milk, stirring vigorously. Let cool before transferring to a pastry bag. Be careful when handling this because it is hotter than the sun.

To assemble

8 Carefully remove the cooled cakes from their pans and peel off the lining paper, keeping the crumble topping facing upward. Place one cake on a cake board or serving plate. Spread the apple puree across the top of the crumble (go gently here or the crumble will come off). **Pipe** splodges of the crème pâtissière over the puree and drizzle with caramel. Stack the remaining cake on top, crumble-side up, and drizzle with more caramel to finish. Any leftover caramel can be used to make Grapefruit Puffs (see page 131).

HONESTLY, CHECK THIS OUT... →

Lemon & Poppy Seed Cake with Elderflower Buttercream

A FACEFUL OF SUMMER

This super-simple, single-tiered cake packs a punch. It's your basic lemon drizzle with a twist, because the elderflower buttercream makes it taste like something you found in the garden. In a good way.

KIT LIST
8-inch round cake pan
stand mixer or electric hand mixer
Microplane
rubber spatula (optional)
toothpick
food processor
metal spatula

For the cake
1 stick unsalted butter, softened, plus extra for greasing
½ cup superfine sugar
4 eggs
zest and juice of 2 lemons, plus extra zest to decorate
⅓ cup ground almonds
2 tablespoons poppy seeds, plus extra to decorate
1 cup all-purpose flour sifted with 2 teaspoons baking powder

For the syrup
juice of 3 lemons
1 tablespoon superfine sugar
½ teaspoon elderflower cordial

For the frosting
1⅓ sticks unsalted butter, softened
1¾ cups powdered sugar
2 teaspoons elderflower cordial

1 Preheat the oven to 350°F. Grease and line the cake pan with parchment paper.

2 Start with the cake. **Cream** the butter and sugar together in a stand mixer or in a large bowl with an electric hand mixer for about 3 minutes. Add the eggs one at a time, beating well after each addition. Add the lemon zest and juice and mix until incorporated.

3 Add the ground almonds and poppy seeds, then sift in the prepared flour. **Fold** in to combine. Transfer the batter to the lined pan and bake for 25 minutes or until golden brown. Remove from the oven and let cool completely in the pan.

4 Meanwhile, make the syrup. Put all the ingredients into a small saucepan. Simmer gently over low heat until the sugar has dissolved, then set aside. Use a toothpick to make little holes all over the top of the cake, then drizzle the top with the syrup.*

5 To make the frosting, cream the ingredients together in a food processor. (This can be done in a stand mixer or a large bowl with an electric hand mixer, but the processor is quickest.)

6 Remove the cake from the pan, peel off the paper, and set on a serving plate. Spread the cake with the frosting using a metal spatula and scatter with lemon zest and some poppy seeds.

* If you get overexcited and the syrup starts to overflow, don't worry. Walk away and don't look at it for a bit. When you come back it will have sorted itself out.

Store in an airtight container in a cool place (not the fridge) for up to 4 days.

Difficulty:

Ultimate Chocolate Cake

This cake does not travel well in the mail. Structural integrity was not top of the list, but the intensely indulgent chocolate hit was. This means it's delicious but also that as many slices as possible should be served in one go, because once the first slice is removed the custard will ooze out and then the cake will probably collapse.

Ideally this cake should be made up of four layers, but you can do it with just two. If you do decide to do all four, there is no need to double the custard or frosting quantities as there will be enough either way.

KIT LIST
2 (or even better, 4) 8-inch round cake pans
hand whisk
electric hand mixer
food processor
round cookie cutter, about 4 inches
cake board (optional)
small metal spatula
pastry bag and tip (optional)

For the cake layers (this makes 2, but you'll want to double it to make 4)
3⅓ cups all-purpose flour
1 cup superfine sugar
½ cup firmly packed soft light brown sugar
½ cup high-quality unsweetened cocoa powder
2 teaspoons baking powder
1 teaspoon baking soda
½ teaspoon salt
3 large eggs
⅔ cup sour cream
1 shot of freshly brewed espresso coffee, cooled
1 tablespoon vanilla bean paste
1½ sticks unsalted butter, melted, plus extra for greasing
½ cup corn oil
1¼ cups ice-cold water

For the custard
5 large egg yolks
⅔ cup superfine sugar
2 tablespoons cornstarch
1 cup milk
1 cup heavy cream
3½ ounces dark (semi-sweet) chocolate (70% cocoa solids minimum), broken into pieces

For the frosting
6¼ ounces dark (semi-sweet) chocolate (70% cocoa solids minimum), broken into pieces
2¼ sticks unsalted butter, softened
2½ cups powdered sugar
2 tablespoons chocolate liqueur (optional)

To decorate
chocolate treats (I like Maltesers, Buttons, Ferrero Rocher...), white chocolate chips and candy sprinkles, to decorate

 This will not keep, so get stuck in.

To make the cake layers

1 Preheat the oven to 350°F. Grease the cake pans and line the bottoms with parchment paper.

2 Mix all the dry ingredients together in a large bowl with a hand whisk until evenly combined.

3 In a separate large bowl, whisk together the eggs, sour cream, cooled coffee, and vanilla paste.

4 Pour the melted butter and oil into YET ANOTHER bowl and beat together well with an electric hand mixer. Dribble the measured water into the bowl while continuing to whisk. This will emulsify the mixture (I don't understand it—ask Prue). Now combine this oil mixture with the egg mixture and beat again. Finally, add this wet mixture to the dry ingredients and whisk until just combined (make sure to include the pesky bits of flour hiding at the bottom of the bowl).

5 Divide the batter equally between the lined pans and bake for 40 minutes, or until a skewer inserted in the middle comes out clean. If you are doubling the cake layer recipe (which I recommend), then get cracking with the ingredients to repeat the process. Remove from the oven and let cool in the pans.

To make the custard

6 While your cake layers are baking, whisk the egg yolks, sugar, and cornstarch together in a bowl with a hand whisk until you have a pale paste. Heat the milk, cream, and chocolate in a medium saucepan over low heat, stirring, until the chocolate has melted and the mixture is steaming but not boiling. Pour a little of the hot milk mixture onto the egg yolk mixture and whisk vigorously to combine, then gradually add half of the remaining hot milk mixture in a thin stream, whisking constantly until it is all incorporated. Add the egg yolk mixture to the pan, place over medium heat, and bring to a boil, whisking constantly until thickened to a custard consistency that you are happy with.

7 Pour the custard through a strainer over a bowl, cover the surface with plastic wrap to stop a skin from forming, and let cool.

To make the frosting

8 Melt the chocolate in a microwave-safe bowl in the microwave using the **heat, stir, repeat** method until smooth, then set aside to cool. Once cooled, put into a food processor with the other frosting ingredients and blitz until creamy. If you don't have a food processor, do it the old-fashioned way, creaming the butter, sifting in the powdered sugar, and then adding the chocolate (and liqueur if using) before beating together.

To assemble

9 Remove your cooled cakes from their pans and peel off the lining paper. Using the cookie cutter, stamp out a circle from the center of one cake if you've made 2, or from 2 cakes if you've made 4. Crumble up the cake circle(s) you've cut out and reserve.

10 Place a complete cake (no hole), bottom-side up, on a cake board or serving plate. Spread a layer of frosting over the top using a small metal spatula, and stack a holey cake, bottom-side up again, on top. Then fill the hole with custard and some of the reserved crumbled cake. Pop some chocolate treats in, too, if you like. If you've made 4 cake layers, spread another layer of frosting on the ring of cake around the hole, then stack with a complete cake before repeating the process so that you finish with a custard-filled hole as the top layer. Fill with more treats and cake crumbs.

11 Decorate the cake with any frosting you have left over (use a pastry bag and fancy tip if you have one) and even more of your favorite treats.

IF YOU'RE NOT ALREADY DRIBBLING... ➔ ➔

Ginger & Coffee Rock Cakes

THEY TASTE BETTER THAN THEY SOUND

These sound ugly and look quite ugly too. They're quite similar to scones and to be honest I can't work out the difference. But they are delicious and crunchy, and the hint of coffee works really nicely with the ginger. A great cake if fiddly decoration isn't really your thing. I wanted to incorporate a rock and roll pun into this intro, but I can't because there is literally no rolling involved.

1 Preheat the oven to 425°F and line a baking sheet with parchment paper.

2 Put the prepared flour into a large bowl, add the butter, and rub in with your fingertips (or blitz in a food processor if you want to make this easy recipe even easier). Add the sugar, ginger, and raisins and stir to combine. Make a **well** in the center and pour in the egg. Stir the egg in the well, gradually picking up the dry mixture from around the well until it is all incorporated. If it feels a little too dry and crumbly, then add a splash of milk. Put 12 lumps (roughly 2 tablespoons of the mixture each) onto your lined cookie sheet. Bake for 10 to 12 minutes until golden, then remove from the oven and let cool completely on the sheet.

3 Meanwhile, make the frosting. **Cream** the ingredients together in a food processor, or in a large bowl with an electric hand mixer.

4 Cut the cakes in half horizontally, spread with frosting and sandwich the two halves back together.* Dust with powdered sugar to serve.

KIT LIST
cookie sheet
food processor or electric hand mixer

For the cakes
1¾ cups all-purpose flour sifted with
   1½ teaspoons baking powder
¾ stick unsalted butter, chilled and cubed
⅓ cup turbinado sugar
¼ cup chopped crystallized ginger
⅓ cup raisins
1 egg, beaten
splash of milk, if needed

For the coffee frosting
3½ tablespoons unsalted butter, softened
1 tablespoon instant coffee dissolved in
   a dash of water to make a paste
⅔ cup powdered sugar, sifted, plus extra
   for dusting

* In the unlikely event that the cakes haven't risen enough to make cutting them in half possible, just slather the frosting on wherever you can, because you don't want to miss out on that flavor.

 Store in an airtight container at room temperature for up to 2 days.

Difficulty:

Banocolatee Bread

BECAUSE BANANA BREAD IS BORING

I tried to make the title of this one snappy by combining banana, chocolate, and toffee into one word, but I'm not sure it will catch on, and I don't even know how to say it. Everyone loves banana bread, blah blah blah—BORING. Give this a try instead. Because chocolate and toffee sauce make everything better...

KIT LIST
6-inch x 3½-inch x 2-inch loaf pan
stand mixer or electric hand mixer
food processor or blender (optional)

For the cake
1 stick unsalted butter, softened
¼ cup superfine sugar
3 overripe bananas, peeled and well mashed
1 egg
1⅔ cups all-purpose flour sifted with
    1½ teaspoons baking powder
3½ ounces dark (semi-sweet) chocolate
    (54% cocoa solids minimum), chopped
    or blitzed to a small rubble in a food
    processor
pinch of salt

For the toffee sauce
⅓ cup firmly packed soft dark brown sugar
⅔ stick unsalted butter
½ tablespoon light corn syrup
⅔ cup heavy cream, plus extra to serve
pinch of salt, or to taste

 Store in an airtight container at room temperature for up to 2 days.

1 Preheat the oven to 400°F and line the loaf pan with parchment paper.

2 For the cake, **cream** the butter and sugar together in a stand mixer or in a bowl with an electric hand mixer for 3 minutes. Add the mashed bananas and combine, then beat in the egg. Sift in the prepared flour, add the chocolate and salt, then **fold** into the mixture. Transfer to the lined pan and bake for about 40 to 45 minutes, or until a skewer inserted into the middle comes out clean.* Let cool while you make the sauce.

3 Melt the sugar, butter, and syrup together in a medium saucepan over medium heat. Bring to a boil and let thicken for a couple of minutes. Stir in the cream and boil for another couple of minutes. Let cool, then add salt to taste.

4 Remove the cake from the pan by inverting it onto a serving plate. Peel off the lining paper and pour the toffee sauce over the top. Best sliced and served warm with a little extra cream on the side.

✱ If the top is starting to burn but the skewer isn't coming out clean, cover loosely with foil and return to the oven. We're trying to avoid the top burning before the middle has cooked. If this does happen, you can just cut off the burned top before serving. Once you've got the sauce on there, nobody will notice or care.

You're Bready for This

Before I went on *Bake Off* I had never made bread before. I taught myself by watching people online and talking to bread heads who knew a lot more than me (so pretty much everyone else in the tent). I think that's reflected in this chapter because I learned to make a basic dough (turns out it's just flour, yeast, water, and a bit of salt) and then just started throwing mad flavors I liked on top of that. Sure, it gets a bit more complicated when you get to enriched doughs, which have a few more ingredients, or different kneading styles. But all of these recipes can be made by a beginner breadmaker. And I know that because I am quite literally a beginner breadmaker.

Start with the soda bread on page 103—it requires no skill whatsoever—then build to some of the more challenging recipes, like the Nacho Bread (pages 110–11) and Sin-amon Rolls (pages 91–2), which are the ultimate crowd-pleasers. People like bread, so people will like you if you learn to make it. Probably.

Difficulty:

Raspberry Butter Buns

WET WIPES HIGHLY RECOMMENDED

**This is a traditional Shropshire bake, brought to my attention by a woman
called Judy, whom I've never actually met (shout out to Judy). I've gone
for raspberry jam, but you can use whatever flavor you like. And while I'm
partial to a big bun, you can make yours a more respectable size. The key
is not to waste any of the sticky caramelized filling that will ooze out of the
buns as they bake. That really is the best bit, so don't leave it on the cookie
sheet to be washed away.**

KIT LIST
hand whisk
electric hand mixer
Microplane (optional)
cookie sheet
pastry brush

For the buns
1¼ cups milk
¼ cup superfine sugar
3½ tablespoons unsalted butter
¼-ounce pack active dry yeast
1 egg
3¼ cups strong white bread flour, plus extra
    for dusting
1¼ cups all-purpose flour
1 teaspoon salt
oil, for greasing

For the raspberry filling
1¾ sticks unsalted butter, softened
1 cup lightly packed soft light brown sugar
¼ cup raspberry jam
zest of 1 lemon

1 For the buns, heat the milk with the sugar in a saucepan over
low heat until steaming but not boiling. Remove from the heat,
add the butter, and stir until melted, then transfer to a small bowl.
Once cool enough to dip your finger in it (and cool enough that
you don't think you'll scramble the egg), add the yeast and then
the egg, and whisk vigorously with a hand whisk until there are
no lumps of yeast visible. Set aside for about 10 minutes until
bubbles form on the surface.

2 Mix the flours and salt together in a large bowl with your hand
whisk. Pour in the yeast mixture and mix everything together with
your hands until a dough is formed.

3 Lightly flour a work surface, turn the dough out onto it, and
knead for 12 to 15 minutes. Grease a large bowl with a little oil
and add the dough. Cover the bowl with plastic wrap and let
prove in a warm place for 2 hours, or until doubled in size.

4 Meanwhile, make the raspberry filling. Beat the butter in a
large bowl until smooth. Add the sugar, **cream** together with an
electric hand mixer, then stir in the jam and lemon zest. Cover the
bowl with plastic wrap and rest in the fridge until needed.

WAIT, THERE'S MORE... ➡️

For the glaze
⅓ cup milk
⅓ cup superfine sugar

5 Once the dough has doubled in size, divide it into 8 pieces and roll each into a ball. Roll the balls flat with a rolling pin into circles and place 1 tablespoon of raspberry filling in the center of each. Fold them in half to make a semicircular shape, ensuring you get any trapped air out before pressing the edges together to seal tightly. Take another tablespoon of the mixture and place it on one half of the semicircle, then fold in half again to make a quarter-circle, removing the air and sealing tightly again.

6 Line a cookie sheet with parchment paper, then set the buns on top. It doesn't matter if the buns are touching as they will join up during the second prove/bake anyway. Cover with plastic wrap and let prove again for 30 minutes.* Meanwhile, preheat the oven to 400°F.

7 To make the glaze, heat the milk and sugar together in a small saucepan, stirring until the sugar has melted (so that you can't feel any grainy bits when you stir it), then set aside.

8 Take off the plastic wrap and bake the buns for 15 to 20 minutes until golden brown. Remove from the oven and brush with the milk glaze. Let stand on the sheet for 15 minutes before serving. And make sure to serve with the sticky bits that will have oozed out the sides—these are the best bits!

✳ Some of the buns will burst open after this second prove. Don't worry about this too much, but if there are any particularly gaping holes, then try to reseal as best you can.

 Store in an airtight container at room temperature for up to 2 days.

Difficulty:

Sin-amon Rolls

THEY'RE THAT GOOD

These are really good. Made with an enriched dough, they're your classic cinnamon rolls with cream cheese frosting, and chocolate and cherry thrown in for good measure. They take time, but it is totally worth it. These are best enjoyed warm, so if you're eating them the morning after the night before, pop them in the microwave for 15 seconds.

KIT LIST
hand whisk
stand mixer and dough hook (optional)
12-inch x 9-inch-deep baking pan
electric hand mixer or food processor
    (optional)

For the rolls
1 cup milk
⅔ stick unsalted butter, plus extra for
    greasing
½ cup superfine sugar
¼-ounce pack active dry yeast
5 cups strong white bread flour, plus extra
    for dusting
1½ teaspoons salt
2 eggs
oil, for greasing

For the filling
⅔ stick unsalted butter, softened
    (spreadable consistency)
1 cup firmly packed soft dark brown sugar
2½ tablespoons ground cinnamon
3½ ounces dark (semi-sweet) chocolate
    (54% cocoa solids minimum), chopped
    into small pieces
¾ cup dried cherries

For the frosting
¾ cup cream cheese
1 stick unsalted butter, softened
pinch of salt
1 tablespoon vanilla bean paste
3¼ cups powdered sugar

1 For the rolls, heat the milk in saucepan over medium heat until steaming but not boiling. Remove from the heat, add the butter, and stir until melted. Add the sugar and mix well, then transfer to a bowl. Once the milk is cool enough to dip your finger into, add the yeast and whisk vigorously with a hand whisk until there are no lumps of yeast visible. Set aside for about 10 minutes until bubbles form on the surface.

2 Mix the flour and salt together in a large bowl with your hand whisk. Then whisk the eggs into the milky yeast mixture in your other bowl before pouring it into the flour. Bring the mixture together with your hands, splaying your fingers rigidly like a claw, until a dough is formed.

3 Lightly flour a work surface, turn the dough out onto it and **knead** for 20 minutes by hand, or knead the dough in a stand mixer fitted with a dough hook for 10 minutes. The mixer is easier, but I get much better results taking the time and doing it by hand.

4 Grease a large bowl with a little oil and add the dough. Cover the bowl with plastic wrap and let **prove** until doubled in size. This normally takes around an hour, depending on how warm the room is.

WAIT, THERE'S MORE...

5 Turn the dough out onto your work surface and use a rolling pin to roll it into a rectangular shape about 20 inches by 16 inches.* Spread the soft butter for the filling across the dough, right to the edges. Sprinkle with the brown sugar and cinnamon, pressing down gently with your hands where needed to make sure it sticks to the butter. Then scatter with the chocolate and cherries and press down again. Starting at one of the shorter edges, roll up the dough into a tight sausage shape, trim the messy ends, and slice the sausage into 12 pieces.

6 Grease the baking pan with butter and add the 12 rolls, placing them snugly next to one another. Cover with plastic wrap and let prove again until doubled in size (this normally takes about an hour).

7 While the rolls finish proving, preheat the oven to 425°F. Remove the plastic wrap and bake for 15 minutes until golden.

8 Meanwhile, make the frosting. Beat the cream cheese and butter together in your stand mixer or in a large bowl with an electric hand mixer, or in a food processor, just until smooth. Beat in the salt and vanilla paste, then sift in the powdered sugar and beat it in. I add it in batches, beating between each addition, to prevent a powdered sugar cloud from coating every surface in the kitchen.

9 Remove the rolls from the oven, spread the frosting over the warm rolls, and let stand for 15 minutes before eating.

✳

Listen, you might find that your rectangle is smaller than this, is wonky, or maybe doesn't even look like a rectangle at all. If that happens, forget the measurements. The most important thing is to focus on rolling the dough out to an even height. You can then trim off the edges to make it into the biggest rectangle possible. Uniformity and shape are more important than size.

Store in an airtight container somewhere cool (preferably not the fridge) for up to 3 days.

Difficulty:

Minimal Faff Brioche

I HAVE A PUBLIC DUTY TO SHARE THIS SACRILEGIOUS BREAD CHEAT

I discovered this method when I was planning to make savarins for *Bake Off*. Not understanding or knowing bread, I was just messing around with the really dry savarin dough and suddenly had a baby brioche on my hands. It's the size that's key, because if you don't use a mini loaf pan or mold you will just have a big dry loaf. That said, I'd rather have a slightly dry brioche to cover in butter than no brioche at all.

KIT LIST

stand mixer and dough hook

pastry bag

6-hole muffin pan, 8-hole mini loaf pan, or 8-cavity cube silicone mold (if using the latter you will end up with miniature loaves)

Ingredients

4 eggs

2 cups all-purpose flour

¼-ounce pack active dry yeast

1 teaspoon salt

2 tablespoons superfine sugar

1 stick unsalted butter, melted and cooled, plus extra to serve

oil, for greasing

marmalade, to serve (optional)

1 Break the eggs into the bowl of a stand mixer and add the flour, yeast, salt, and sugar. **Knead** with the dough hook attachment for 10 minutes. While continuing to knead, gradually add one-third of the melted butter. When the butter has stopped sloshing around and has become part of the dough, repeat with the next third and then the final third.* Continue to knead for about 15 minutes.

2 Grease a bowl with oil and add the dough. Cover with plastic wrap and let **prove** in a warm place for an hour, or until doubled in size.

3 While the dough finishes proving, preheat the oven to 410°F.

4 Transfer the dough to a pastry bag, cut the tip off, and **pipe** into a muffin pan or similar. You want to half-fill each hole to allow space for baking. Lightly oil a piece of plastic wrap, cover the pan or mold with the plastic wrap, oiled-side down, and let the dough prove again for 15 minutes.

5 Take off the plastic wrap and bake the brioche for 15 minutes. Remove from the oven, then transfer the brioche to a wire rack to cool. Serve warm with butter and marmalade, or slice and broil to make great Melba toast.

* If your butter is not incorporating into the dough, stop the mixer, scrape down the sides, and try mixing by hand for a while to get it going.

 Store in an airtight container at room temperature for up to 4 days.

Difficulty:

Big Daddy's Ice Cream Doughnut Sandwiches

CHURNING & FRYING NOT NECESSARY

Doughnuts are the best, but really hard to make if you don't have a deep-fat fryer. Well, not anymore, because these doughnuts are baked rather than fried. And, because once you've started cheating it's hard to stop, why not serve these with really simple no-churn ice cream? No fancy equipment necessary. The doughnuts take at least 2 hours to prove and the ice cream needs around an hour to freeze, but all good things come to those who wait.

KIT LIST
hand whisk
stand mixer and dough hook (optional)
cookie sheet
pastry brush
Microplane (optional)
electric hand mixer
large freezer container with lid, chilled

For the doughnuts
1¼ cups milk
5½ tablespoons unsalted butter
¼ cup superfine sugar
¼-ounce pack active dry yeast
4 cups strong white bread flour,
   plus extra for dusting
1 teaspoon salt
1 egg
olive oil, for greasing
⅓ cup superfine sugar, for coating

For the ice cream
14-ounce can condensed milk
1 tablespoon vanilla bean paste
zest of 1 lemon
pinch of salt
2 cups heavy cream

For the raspberry coulis
2½ cups fresh raspberries
juice of ½ lemon
2 tablespoons Chambord (optional)

Once assembled, these need to be eaten straightaway. But, if you want to, you can make the different components in advance: the ice cream will be fine if kept in the freezer; the coulis will keep in the fridge for a couple of days, and the doughnuts can be made a day in advance and kept in an airtight container at room temperature.

To make the doughnuts

1 Heat the milk in a saucepan over medium heat until steaming but not boiling. Remove from the heat, add 3½ tablespoons of the butter, and stir until melted. Add the superfine sugar and mix well, then transfer to a bowl. Once the mixture is cool enough to dip your finger in it, add the yeast and whisk vigorously with a hand whisk until there are no lumps of yeast visible. Set aside for about 10 minutes until bubbles form on the surface.

2 Mix the flour and salt together in a large bowl with your hand whisk. Then whisk the egg into the yeast mixture before pouring it into the flour. Mix everything together with your hands until a dough is formed.

3 Lightly flour a work surface, turn the dough out onto it, and **knead** for 15 minutes by hand, or knead the dough in a stand mixer fitted with a dough hook for 8 minutes.

4 Grease a large bowl with a little olive oil and add the dough. Cover the bowl with plastic wrap and let **prove** in a warm place for about an hour, or until doubled in size. At this stage you could crack on and make the ice cream (see right).

5 Oil a cookie sheet. Turn the dough out onto a lightly floured work surface and **knock back** by flattening it with your fist. Divide the dough into 3-ounce balls. Place on the oiled cookie sheet with a sizable gap between each one. Cover with plastic wrap and let prove again for about an hour, or until doubled in size. Meanwhile, preheat the oven to 375°F and place a roasting pan filled with water into the bottom of it.

6 Take off the plastic wrap, place the sheet of doughnuts on the middle shelf of the oven, and bake for about 12 minutes until golden brown.

7 Meanwhile, melt the remaining 2 tablespoons butter and spread the superfine sugar out on a cookie sheet. Remove the doughnuts from the oven, brush them with the butter, and then roll in the sugar, making sure each one is well coated. Set aside to cool. While the doughnuts are cooling, make the raspberry coulis and, if you haven't already done so, the ice cream (see right).

To make the ice cream

8 Mix all the ingredients apart from the cream together in a bowl.

9 In a separate bowl, whip the cream with an electric hand mixer until it holds its shape (**stiff peaks**).* Add a large spoonful of the whipped cream to the other bowl and stir well until incorporated and smooth. Then pour this mixture into the rest of the whipped cream and mix together until no lumps remain. Now add this to the chilled freezer container. Spread it out evenly, cover with the lid, and place in the freezer for a minimum of an hour.

To make the raspberry coulis

10 Put the raspberries, lemon juice, and a splash of water into a medium saucepan, mash, and bring to a boil. Once the mixture starts to **reduce**, add the Chambord (if using) and return to a boil.

11 Remove from the heat and pour the mixture through a sieve into a small bowl to remove the seeds.

To assemble

12 Halve the doughnuts, add a scoop of the ice cream, drizzle with the coulis, and sandwich together.

* If you've overwhipped the cream, it is going to be very difficult to turn it into a smooth ice cream. But don't panic. Add a little of your heavy cream and mix in by hand until the mixture softens. Worst-case scenario, you'll end up churning yourself some homemade butter, in which case just enjoy it on some toast.

LOOK, THERE'S A PICTURE... ➔ ➔

Difficulty:

Blackberry & White Chocolate Muffins

BECAUSE YOU'RE WORTH IT

This muffin recipe really has earned its place. The cream cheese spreads through the muffins to make them reminiscent of cheesecake in flavor, while the blackberry keeps them nice and moist. You could swap in another berry, but I think blackberries look cool. Because they're my favorite color. Shocker. Mastered this? See page 121 for a savory muffin recipe.

KIT LIST
rubber spatula (optional)
Microplane (optional)
9-hole muffin pan (if you only have a 6-hole muffin pan, you can bake in 2 batches)
9 muffin cups or large baking cups

Ingredients
2 eggs
⅓ cup plain yogurt
⅓ cup cream cheese
4 teaspoons milk
1⅔ cups all-purpose flour sifted with 2½ teaspoons baking powder
½ teaspoon salt
½ cup superfine sugar
3½ ounces white chocolate, chopped
zest of 1 lemon
⅔ cup fresh blackberries, chopped

1 Put the eggs, yogurt, cream cheese, and milk into a large liquid measuring cup and whisk together with a fork until combined.

2 Sift the prepared flour and the salt together into a bowl, then stir in the sugar and white chocolate.

3 Pour the wet ingredients into the dry ingredients, add the lemon zest and chopped blackberries, and **fold** together, being careful not to overmix and stopping as soon as there is no dry flour visible. Cover the bowl with plastic wrap and let the batter rest in the fridge for an hour.

4 While the batter finishes resting, preheat the oven to 400°F and line the pan with the cups.*

5 Once the batter has rested, take it out of the fridge and fill each cup to just under the lip of the pan. Bake for 20 to 25 minutes until golden brown on top.

6 Remove from the oven and let the muffins cool completely in the pan before serving.

Store in an airtight container at room temperature for up to 3 days.

* It might be worth putting a little oil on some paper towels and lightly greasing the top of the pan. When the muffins rise, they form the infamous "muffin tops," which can make them a little tricky to get out if the pan isn't greased!

Difficulty:

Brown Bread with Bits In

LIKE SEEDS AND STUFF

A simple loaf to have as your in-house healthy bread for toast, sandwiches etc. I throw in some seeds, but add whatever you fancy. While possible to make by hand, the kneading is intense, so use a stand mixer fitted with a dough hook if you have one.

KIT LIST
hand whisk
stand mixer and dough hook (optional)
9-inch x 5-inch x 3-inch loaf pan
pastry brush

Ingredients
1 cup warm water
¼-ounce pack active dry yeast
1 tablespoon honey
3½ cups strong whole-wheat or seeded bread flour, plus extra for dusting
1 teaspoon salt
oil, for greasing and brushing
2 tablespoons sunflower seeds
1 tablespoon sesame seeds
1 tablespoon poppy seeds

 Store however you normally store your bread.

1 Put the measured warm water, yeast, and honey into a small bowl and whisk vigorously together with a hand whisk until there are no lumps of yeast visible. Set aside for about 10 minutes until bubbles form on the surface.

2 Mix the flour and salt together in a large bowl with your hand whisk. Pour in the yeast mixture and mix everything together with your hands until a dough is formed.

3 Lightly flour a work surface, turn the dough out onto it and **knead** for 15 minutes by hand, or knead the dough in a stand mixer fitted with a dough hook for 10 minutes. This will be stiffer and drier than any other bread dough in this book because of the whole-wheat flour, but hang in there and keep working it.

4 Grease a large bowl with a little oil and add the dough. Cover the bowl with plastic wrap and let **prove** in a warm place until doubled in size (I leave mine for an hour at this stage).

5 Turn the dough out onto a lightly floured work surface and **knock back** into a rough rectangle, spread it out with your fingertips, and scatter with the seeds. Roll the bread up and then work the seeds through the dough until evenly distributed.* Now roll it up into a fat sausage. Oil the pan and transfer the dough to it. Cover with plastic wrap and let prove again for an hour.

6 While your dough finishes proving, preheat the oven to 400°F. Once the dough has proved, remove the plastic wrap and brush a little oil on the top. Use a sharp knife to make some diagonal cuts across the top. This makes it look like bread you'd find in a bakery *and* stops it from splitting down the sides. Bake for 35 minutes, then remove from the oven and tip the loaf out of the pan. Set the loaf directly on the oven shelf and bake for another 10 minutes.

7 Remove from the oven and let cool completely on a wire rack before slicing.

> ✳ Finding it too hard to work the seeds into the dough? Forget about it and move on. Then, before you put the loaf in for its final 10 minutes of baking, brush the top with a little oil and sprinkle on some seeds. Do this any sooner and they are likely to burn.

Difficulty:

Build-A-Bread

SODA BREAD FOR YOU TO PUT YOUR STAMP ON

You can sort this bread out in about an hour because it's really easy and literally has nothing to prove (get it?). I've included some of my favorite flavors here, but think of this recipe as a blank canvas, so be as creative as you like with what you chuck into it. You might make something disgusting or it might be a triumph, but there's only one way to find out...

KIT LIST
hand whisk
cookie sheet

Ingredients
2 tablespoons unsalted butter, plus extra to serve (optional)
2 red onions, thinly sliced
good glug of balsamic vinegar
4 cups all-purpose flour, plus extra for dusting
1 teaspoon baking soda
1 teaspoon salt
1 teaspoon dried oregano
1 teaspoon smoked paprika
½ teaspoon chili flakes (optional)
4 ounces chorizo sausage, skinned and finely chopped
¼ cup chopped pitted black olives (optional, but to be honest, all these ingredients are optional apart from the flour, baking soda, and buttermilk)
1¾ cups buttermilk (you can also use plain yogurt, sour cream, or even milk with 1 tablespoon lemon juice or malt vinegar added to sour it)
freshly ground black pepper
½ cup grated smoked cheddar cheese

1 Preheat the oven to 410°F.

2 Melt the butter in a skillet until just starting to bubble, add the onions, and fry over low heat, stirring regularly, until softened (you don't want to brown them). Add the balsamic and **reduce** until the onions are sticky, then remove from the heat.

3 Put the flour, baking soda, salt, herbs, and spices into a large bowl and mix together with a hand whisk. Add the chorizo, olives, and fried onions and stir to ensure the bits are evenly distributed. Mix in the buttermilk and season with black pepper.

4 Flour your work surface and turn the dough mixture out onto it. Sprinkle it with a little more flour if it is very sticky, then use your hands to bring the dough together, handling it as little as possible. Scatter a cookie sheet with a little flour and transfer the dough onto it. Form it into a round shape, then score a deep cross into the dough and fill the cross with the grated smoked cheddar. Bake for 40 to 45 minutes. You will know it is done if the bread sounds hollow when tapped on the bottom.

5 Remove from the oven and transfer to a wire rack so that it doesn't get a sweaty bottom. Once cool, it is ready to eat. I serve mine with lots of butter.

 Store in an airtight container at room temperature for up to 3 days.

Difficulty:

Cheese/Cinnamon Pretzels

THIS IS AN "OR" NOT AN "AND" SITUATION

Who doesn't love a pretzel? Once you've got your head around enriched dough, you'll be making these nonstop. They can be sweet or savory. I've gone for cheese or cinnamon, but you do you.

KIT LIST
hand whisk
2 cookie sheets
slotted spoon
pastry brush

For the dough
⅔ cup warm water
⅔ cup warm milk
¼-ounce pack active dry yeast
1 tablespoon light corn syrup or
    1½ tablespoons superfine sugar
3½ cups strong white bread flour,
    plus extra for dusting
1 teaspoon salt
oil, for greasing
3 tablespoons baking soda
1 egg, beaten, for **egg wash**

For savory cheese pretzels
¾ cup grated cheddar cheese
sweet chutney, to serve

1 To make the pretzel dough, put the measured warm water, milk, and yeast into a small bowl and whisk vigorously together with a hand whisk until there are no lumps of yeast visible. Add the light corn syrup or superfine sugar and whisk again. Set aside for about 10 minutes until bubbles form on the surface.

2 Mix the flour and salt together in a large bowl with your hand whisk. Pour in the yeast mixture and stir it in, then use your hands to work the mixture into a dough.

3 Lightly flour a work surface, turn the dough out onto it and **knead** for a minimum of 15 minutes until smooth. This is where you can use the famed **windowpane test** to see if it is ready to **prove**.

4 Grease a large bowl with a little oil and plop the dough in. Cover the bowl with plastic wrap and let prove in a warm place for an hour, or until doubled in size. Meanwhile, line your cookie sheets with parchment paper.

5 Divide the proved dough into 12 equal-sized balls and then roll each one into a long, thin rope, ideally about 16 inches in length (don't lose sleep over the length; if yours are shorter, you will just have smaller pretzels).

6 To make the traditional pretzel shape, bring the ends of one rope together as if making a circle, cross them over and join the ends to the shoulder of the pretzel by pressing firmly together. Don't feel limited to this shape though. You can make anything that doesn't have a loose end (think figure eights, stars, hearts, whatever... just get creative). Place your pretzels on the lined cookie sheets. Lightly oil 2 pieces of plastic wrap, cover the cookie sheets with the plastic wrap, oiled-side down, and let the pretzels prove again for 30 minutes.

For sweet cinnamon pretzels
3½ tablespoons unsalted butter, melted
superfine sugar and ground cinnamon,
  mixed—I'm not prescribing quantities
  here because it is personal preference,
  but I use about ⅓ cup sugar with
  1 tablespoon ground cinnamon
melted chocolate, to serve (optional)

7 Preheat the oven to 400°F. Bring a big pot of water, about 2 quarts, to a boil and add the baking soda. Take off the plastic wrap and lower your pretzels into the boiling water one at a time, keeping them in there for no more than 30 seconds and flipping halfway through. Remove from the water with a slotted spoon and return to the cookie sheets.*

8 Brush the pretzels lightly with **egg wash** and bake for 15 to 20 minutes until golden brown. If making cheese pretzels, sprinkle them with grated cheddar after they have been baking for 10 minutes, and then return to the oven to finish baking.

9 Remove from the oven and let cool for 10 minutes on the sheets. For cinnamon pretzels, brush with the melted butter and then roll in the cinnamon sugar. Serve these with melted chocolate for a truly decadent finish. The cheese pretzels should be served with a sweet chutney of some sort. I use my mom's onion chutney (which she won't give me the recipe for).

＊ At some point in this process, one or more of your pretzels might lose their shape. Once you've put them on the cookie sheet post boil, wait for them to be cool enough to touch (which won't take long) and just pinch any loose ends together, abandoning the original shape. It's more important that there are no breaks (unless you want a breadstick).

AS IF YOU DON'T WANT TO EAT THESE... ➔ ➔

 Store in an airtight container at room temperature for up to 2 days. The cinnamon pretzels will eventually get soggy, as they are covered in butter, so better to eat those sooner rather than later.

Difficulty:

Sun-dried Tomato & Olive Sticks

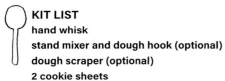
OLIVE, LAUGH, LOVE

I'd call these breadsticks but those bring back too many bad memories of stale snacks at parties. They're also not really baguettes, although they could be used to make a really, really narrow sandwich with not much filling. Let's just stick with sticks.

KIT LIST
hand whisk
stand mixer and dough hook (optional)
dough scraper (optional)
2 cookie sheets

Ingredients
1 cup warm water
¼-ounce pack active dry yeast
1 tablespoon honey
2¾ cups strong white bread flour,
    plus extra for dusting
1 teaspoon salt
2 tablespoons olive oil
½ cup pitted black or green olives,
    quartered
½ cup chopped sun-dried tomatoes
2 teaspoons dried mixed herbs
oil, for greasing
hummus, to serve (optional)

1 Put the measured warm water, yeast, and honey into a small bowl and whisk vigorously together with a hand whisk until there are no lumps of yeast visible. Set aside for about 10 minutes until bubbles form on the surface.

2 Add the remaining ingredients to the bowl of a stand mixer fitted with a dough hook, then pour in the yeast mixture and **knead** for 10 minutes. You can do this by hand, but beware: it is a very sticky dough, so you will need a well-floured work surface and ideally a dough scraper to help you get it off said surface.

3 Grease a large bowl with oil. Once kneaded, if using a stand mixer, flour your hands before lifting the dough out. Add the dough to the oiled bowl, cover the bowl with plastic wrap, and let **prove** in a warm place for an hour, or until doubled in size.

4 Sprinkle the cookie sheets with flour. Flour your work surface, turn the dough out onto it, and **knock back** using your fingertips. Divide the dough into 2½-ounce balls and roll each one into a sausage shape about 8 inches long. Place on the cookie sheets, cover with plastic wrap, and let prove again for 30 minutes.

5 Preheat the oven to 400°F. Bake the sticks for 10 to 12 minutes until golden brown.* Remove from the oven and let cool on the sheets before serving. These are good with hummus.

Store in an airtight container at room temperature for up to 3 days.

* If they're starting to catch on top but are still a bit undercooked and floppy, flip them over.

Difficulty:

Nacho Bread

SPICE UP YOUR LOAF

Your friends are over. You're watching the game. Someone asks for nachos. You don't have nachos. But you do have a loaf of bread that tastes like nachos. You bring it out for some tearing and sharing. The crowd goes wild.

KIT LIST
**8-inch round, deep, loose-bottomed cake pan
hand whisk**

For the bread dough
butter, for greasing
4 cups strong white bread flour, plus extra
   for dusting
¼-ounce pack active dry yeast
1 tablespoon olive oil, plus extra for greasing
1 teaspoon dried mixed herbs
2 teaspoons taco seasoning
1 teaspoon salt
1⅓ cups warm water
oil, for greasing

For the tomato sauce
2 sun-dried tomatoes, chopped, plus
   1 tablespoon oil from the tomatoes
4 garlic cloves, crushed
pinch of salt
1½ cups tomato puree
1 teaspoon soft light brown sugar
dash of Tabasco sauce

For the fillings
7 ounce jar of jalapeño peppers, drained
   and chopped
1½ cups grated sharp cheddar cheese,
   plus extra for sprinkling on top
¾ cup mascarpone cheese
guacamole, to serve

1 Grease the pan with butter.

2 Put the flour, yeast, oil, herbs, and taco seasoning into a large bowl and mix together with a hand whisk. Add the salt and then gradually add the measured warm water, using your hands with your fingers rigidly splayed like a claw (this will give you the best mix) to combine into a ball of dough. You might not have to use all the water, so just add a little at a time until a dough is formed.

3 Flour your work surface, turn the dough out onto it, and **knead** for 10 to 15 minutes. After a while, the dough will stop sticking to the surface and it will become easier to work with.

4 Grease a large bowl with a little oil and pop the dough into it. Cover the bowl with plastic wrap and let **prove** in a warm place for an hour, or until doubled in size.

5 While your dough is proving, make the tomato sauce. Heat the sun-dried tomato oil in a saucepan over low heat, add the garlic, sun-dried tomatoes, and salt. Fry for a couple of minutes. Add the tomato puree and bring to a boil, then stir in the sugar and Tabasco. Simmer for about 5 minutes, then let cool.

6 Lightly flour your work surface, turn the dough out onto it, and **knock back**. Divide the dough into 12 equal-sized balls and then flatten each one into a disk with your hands. Spoon some tomato sauce onto one dough disk, then add a little of the jalapeños, cheddar, and 1 teaspoon mascarpone. Bring the edges of the disk together around the mixture to form into a ball in the palm of your hand. Gently roll the ball in your hands to smooth any edges and to ensure the filling is well contained. Place the ball in your pan and repeat with the other dough disks and fillings.

7 Once you have a layer of dough balls in the bottom of the pan, cover with tomato sauce and sprinkle with grated cheddar (reserve a little cheese for sprinkling on top later). Place any remaining balls on top.*

8 Cover the pan with plastic wrap and let prove again for an hour.

9 While the dough finishes proving, preheat the oven to 400°F. Once the dough has proved, take off the plastic wrap and bake for 30 minutes. Remove from the oven and sprinkle with the reserved grated cheddar, then bake for an additional 10 minutes. Let cool in the pan for 10 minutes before turning out and serving with a guacamole dip.

✱ If some of your balls are sticking out over the top, don't worry, it just means you'll end up with crispy edges. If the pan looks too crowded, consider transferring them to a larger pan. Any shape is fine, just make sure you always have at least two layers of stacked balls.

SEE HOW TO FILL YOUR BALLS...

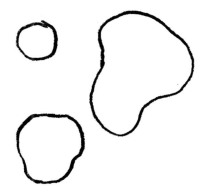

Try to eat once made because this won't store well.

Chili & Garlic Loaf

RED BREAD REDEMPTION

This spicy little number is a basic bread recipe with some solid flavors thrown in. Have it out on the table when you've got people around for something like a chile. Or toast it and eat it by yourself. You can turn up or tone down the heat depending on your audience and how much of a surprise you want to give them. This loaf works particularly well for the Cheese Dream recipe on page 211.

KIT LIST
hand whisk
stand mixer and dough hook (optional)
6-inch x 3½-inch x 2-inch loaf pan

For the bread dough
3¾ cups strong white bread flour,
  plus extra for dusting
2 teaspoons salt
¼-ounce pack active dry yeast
1 tablespoon smoked paprika
8 large garlic cloves, crushed
1 teaspoon chili flakes
1⅓ cups warm water
oil, for greasing

For the filling
1 stick unsalted butter, softened
2 fresh red chilies, finely chopped
2 fresh green chilies, finely chopped
4 large garlic cloves, crushed
1 teaspoon chili flakes
salt and freshly ground black pepper

1 Put the dough ingredients, except the water, into a large bowl. Mix together with a hand whisk. Gradually pour in the measured warm water, mixing with a spoon until a dough starts to form.

2 Flour a work surface, turn the dough out onto it, and **knead** for 10 minutes by hand, or knead the dough in a stand mixer fitted with a dough hook for 8 minutes.

3 Grease a large bowl with a little oil and add the dough. Cover the bowl with plastic wrap and let **prove** in a warm place for about an hour, or until doubled in size.

4 Meanwhile, make the filling. Mix all the ingredients together in a small bowl, seasoning with salt and pepper. Set aside. Line the loaf pan with parchment paper.

5 Flour your work surface, turn the dough out onto it, and **knock back**. Divide the dough into 18 equal-sized portions. Take one portion and roll it out to a square roughly the same size as the short sides of your loaf pan. Spread some of the filling on top and set aside. Repeat with a second portion of dough. Lay this square on top of the first. Repeat until you have a stack of 9 squares. Stand the stack up and transfer it to the pan, pushing it up against one end. The pan should be half filled. Place a glass inside the pan to hold the stack upright while you roll out, spread and stack the remaining dough portions. Remove the glass from the pan and stand the second stack up against the first, filling the pan. Lightly oil a piece of plastic wrap, cover the pan with it, oiled-side down, and let prove again for 30 minutes.

6 Preheat the oven to 400°F. Take off the plastic wrap and bake the loaf for 35 minutes until risen and golden. Remove from the oven, carefully lift out of the pan using the paper,* and let cool on a wire rack before slicing.

* If your loaf is brown and cooked on the top but a bit too soft on the sides, remove the paper and bake on a cookie sheet (out of the pan) for another 10 minutes to crisp up.

Store in an airtight container at room temperature for up to 3 days.

Difficulty:

Calzagne

BECAUSE MAKING DECISIONS IS HARD

Why should we be made to choose between lasagne and pizza? I have no issue with carbs on carbs, so this recipe actually uses lasagne sheets on pizza (but you can leave this out if you really want to). You could eat this as a flat pizza, but I prefer to serve it as a calzone. Is it confusing to eat? Yeah, it is. But is it delicious? I think so.

KIT LIST
hand whisk
small food processor (optional)
2 cookie sheets

For the pizza dough
2¾ cups strong white bread flour, plus extra
    for dusting
¼-ounce pack active dry yeast
1 teaspoon dried mixed herbs
1 teaspoon superfine sugar
1 teaspoon salt
3 tablespoons olive oil, plus extra for greasing
¾ cup warm water

For the cheese sauce
2 tablespoons unsalted butter
3 tablespoons all-purpose flour
1¼ cups milk
freshly ground black pepper
1¼ cups grated sharp cheddar cheese

For the ragù
1 red onion, chopped
2 garlic cloves, chopped
1 carrot, peeled and chopped
½ teaspoon salt
1 tablespoon olive oil
9 ounces pasture-raised ground pork (5% fat)
9 ounces ground beef (5% fat)
3 tablespoons red wine
1 cup beef stock (1 stock pot capsule or cube
    dissolved in 1 cup water)
1 cup tomato puree
1 tablespoon tomato paste
1 teaspoon dried mixed herbs
splash of Worcestershire sauce
freshly ground black pepper

For the filling
4 sheets of fresh lasagne
2 balls of mozzarella cheese, about 4½ ounces each
walnut-sized lump of butter, melted

 **Store in the fridge for up to 2 days
and reheat before serving.**

To make the dough

1 Put the flour, yeast, herbs, and sugar into a large bowl and mix together with a hand whisk. Add the salt and olive oil, then gradually pour in the measured warm water, mixing with a spoon until a sticky dough starts to form.

2 Grease a work surface and a large bowl with a little olive oil. Turn the dough out onto the oiled surface and **knead** for about 5 minutes. Place in the oiled bowl, cover the bowl with plastic wrap, and let **prove** in a warm place for 1½ hours, or until doubled in size.

3 Turn the dough out onto a clean, lightly floured work surface and **knock back**, then return it to the bowl and cover with the plastic wrap again while you make the other elements.

To make the cheese sauce

4 Melt the butter in a medium saucepan over medium heat, add the flour, and **cook out**, stirring constantly. Add the milk a tablespoon at a time, stirring vigorously. Keep adding the milk and stirring until the mixture turns from a paste to the consistency of heavy cream. Bring to a boil, stirring constantly, and boil for about 2 minutes. Remove from the heat, season with black pepper, and add the cheddar, stirring until it has melted. Pour the sauce into a bowl and cover with plastic wrap, making sure it is loose enough for you to press it down across the surface of the sauce to stop a skin from forming.

To make the ragù

5 Blitz the onion, garlic, carrot, and salt together in a small food processor (if you don't have one, then chop really finely). Tip into a large pan with the oil and fry over medium heat until softened. Add the ground meats and fry, breaking them up with a wooden spoon, until evenly browned. Pour in the red wine and stock, bring to a boil, and cook for about 15 minutes. Stir in the remaining ingredients, add black pepper to taste, and cook for another 5 minutes. Remove from the heat and let cool.

To assemble

6 Preheat the oven to 500°F, or as hot as it will go. Grease the cookie sheets with oil.

7 Cook the sheets of lasagne in a large pan of boiling water for about 5 minutes, or until soft. Drain well and set aside. Slice the mozzarella (I aim to get about 8 slices from a ball).

8 When ready to shape and fill the calzagne, lightly flour your work surface and turn the dough out onto it. Divide the dough into 4 equal portions and roll each out into a thin circle. This is tricky because the dough is naturally very elastic, but stick with it and make it as evenly thin as possible. Transfer your first circle to one of the greased cookie sheets to fill. They are harder to move once filled (aren't we all?).

9 Spread one-quarter of the ragù over half of the circle. Top with a sheet of lasagne, followed by one-quarter of the cheese sauce, then add 4 mozzarella slices. Fold in half to seal and **crimp** tightly.* Brush with melted butter. Repeat for the other 3 calzagne.

10 Bake for 15 to 18 minutes until golden brown.

✳ If you aren't feeling great about your **crimping**, or think you have overfilled your calzagnes, cook them seal-side down to minimize the risk of them bursting open. If they do, don't panic, just enjoy the ooze of mozzarella and try harder next time.

SOUNDS HARD, LOOKS EASY... ➔ ➔

Sneaky Cheese Scones

YOU'LL EITHER LOVE THEM OR HATE THEM

Sneaky due to the secret ingredient—yeast extract. For the haters, it is only there to bring out the flavor of the cheese; you won't notice it, I promise. For the lovers, add a bit more to give the scones that kick. These are super simple and you can put them anywhere—in your mouth, in the microwave to reheat, in the freezer for another day, or in the trash if you don't like them.

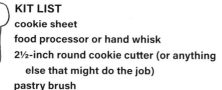

KIT LIST
cookie sheet
food processor or hand whisk
2½-inch round cookie cutter (or anything else that might do the job)
pastry brush

Ingredients
1 stick unsalted butter, chilled and cubed, plus extra for greasing and to serve
2½ cups all-purpose flour sifted with 1 tablespoon baking powder; plus extra flour for dusting
1 teaspoon salt
pinch of freshly ground black pepper
1¼ cups finely grated sharp cheddar cheese
½ cup milk
2 eggs
2 teaspoons yeast extract (I use Marmite. Look it up. It isn't the same thing as yeast.)
1 teaspoon English mustard (optional)

1 Preheat the oven to 425°F and grease a cookie sheet.

2 Blitz the prepared flour, salt, and black pepper in a food processor. Add the butter and blitz again. (If you don't have a food processor, use a hand whisk to combine the dry ingredients in a large bowl, then rub the butter into the flour mixture with your fingertips.) Transfer to a large bowl and stir in 1 cup of the grated cheddar.

3 Whisk the milk, one of the eggs, the yeast extract, and mustard together (if using) in a small bowl or liquid measuring cup, then pour into the flour mixture. Using your hands, bring everything together to form a dough.

4 Lightly flour a work surface, turn the dough out onto it, and pat into a flat circle about 1 inch in thickness.*

5 Beat the remaining egg with a fork. Use the cookie cutter (or alternative) to stamp out as many scones as you can from the circle and place on your greased cookie sheet. Repeat the patting down and stamping-out process until you have no dough left. Brush the tops with the beaten egg and scatter with them with the remaining cheddar.

6 Bake for 15 to 20 minutes until golden brown on top. Remove the scones from the oven and let cool for a bit before serving warm, slathered in butter.

✳ DO NOT overwork the dough here. Touch it as little as possible when shaping.

 Store in an airtight container at room temperature for up to 4 days.

Difficulty:

Pesto Muffins

The perfect picnic snacks—cheesy, pesto muffins with a lovely cakey texture. I don't know if you're supposed to put anything on muffins, but I cover mine in lots of butter when they're fresh out of the oven.

KIT LIST
hand whisk
rubber spatula (optional)
6-hole muffin pan
pastry brush

Ingredients
¼ cup sunflower oil
1 egg
⅔ cup plain yogurt
4 teaspoons milk
2 tablespoons fresh, good-quality pesto*
¾ cup grated sharp cheddar cheese
handful of fresh chives, finely chopped
1⅔ cups all-purpose flour sifted with
   1 tablespoon baking powder; plus
   extra flour for dusting
1 teaspoon salt
1 teaspoon cracked black pepper
   (that's about 6 twists of a grinder)
melted butter or oil, for greasing
butter, to serve

1 Put the oil, egg, yogurt, and milk into a large bowl and whisk together with a hand whisk. Add the pesto, cheddar, and chives and whisk again to combine.

2 Sift the prepared flour and salt together into a separate large bowl, then stir in the cracked black pepper.

3 Pour the wet ingredients into the dry ingredients and **fold** together, being careful not to overmix and stopping as soon as there is no dry flour visible. Cover the bowl with plastic wrap and let the batter rest in the fridge for an hour.

4 While the batter finishes resting, preheat the oven to 400°F. Brush the holes of the muffin pan with a little melted butter or oil, making sure to reach down into the bottom of each hole. Sprinkle a little flour into the holes, then tap and rotate the pan to ensure each hole is lightly coated all the way up in flour. This will make the muffins easier to get out later.

5 Divide the batter evenly between the 6 holes of the pan so that they are full, then scrape across the tops so that they are smooth. Bake for 25 to 30 minutes until golden brown on top.

6 Remove from the oven and let cool for 5 minutes in the pan before transferring to a wire rack.

* Strengths of pesto can vary, so you may want to experiment with quantities to get the balance of flavors right.

Store in an airtight container at room temperature for up to 3 days. These freeze well.

Don't Be Scared of Pastry

What I love about pastry is its versatility. There are loads of different types, so as a starting point I have given you basic recipes for four of the most popular, along with some ideas for how to use them. I think the reason pastry feels scary is because of the endless rules: "keep it cold"; "don't let it cool down"; "blind bake it to avoid a soggy bottom," etc. And half the time these rules can seem contradictory. So let's get some basics clear.

For shortcrust pastry (pie dough) and puff pastry of any description—KEEP IT COLD.

For hot water crust—USE IT WHEN IT'S WARM (see what I mean about contradictory rules).

Then you've got choux, which is unlike any other pastry. It has an entirely different set of rules, a load of unnecessary vocabulary and TEMPERATURE DOESN'T MATTER.

Personal favorite from this chapter is the Little Maple Pecan Pies recipe on page 132. My PB is eating six in one sitting, and I challenge (but do not encourage) anyone to beat that.

> * For savory shortcrust pastry (pie dough) follow the recipe below but make three crucial ingredient changes: no powdered sugar, just one egg yolk, and a bit less butter (use 1 stick).

(Sweet*) Shortcrust Pastry

YOU MAY KNOW THIS DOUGH FROM: STRAWBERRY TARTS AND APPLE PIE

This is an incredibly simple way of making shortcrust pastry (pie dough). You just chuck everything into a food processor. The only thing you need to get down is how much water you need to achieve the right consistency. You'll learn to do this instinctively over time. If you don't have a food processor, it's still easy enough. Just be sure to use only your fingertips because they are the coolest part of your hands. In terms of temperature. Opposable thumbs are also cool.

KIT LIST
food processor (optional)

Ingredients
1⅔ cups all-purpose flour, plus extra for dusting
1½ sticks unsalted butter, chilled and cubed
½ cup powdered sugar
pinch of salt
2 egg yolks
1 to 2 teaspoons ice-cold water, only if needed

 Store in the fridge until ready to use, for up to 3 days.

1 Put the flour, butter, powdered sugar, and salt into a food processor. Blitz until the mixture looks like medium breadcrumbs. Add the yolks one at a time, pulsing after each addition. To make by hand, put the flour, powdered sugar, and salt into a bowl, add the butter, and rub in with your fingertips until the mixture looks like medium breadcrumbs. Beat the egg yolks together, then gradually mix in.

2 If the mixture already looks like a dough is forming (i.e., there are large clumps in the food processor or bowl), then you don't need to add water. If it still looks a little floury and dry, add 1 teaspoon of ice-cold water and pulse or mix again. Repeat if needed, but DO NOT make a paste.

3 Lightly flour a work surface, turn the dough out onto it, and bring together into a ball with your hands. Seal in plastic wrap and chill in the fridge for a minimum of 30 minutes before using.

> There is a high butter content in this dough and that is what is going to screw you over. If it gets warm it will feel like you're working with playdough and everything will melt in the oven. So remember, anything buttery likes the cold. Cold hands, cold surface, cold heart...

Hot Water Crust Pastry

YOU MAY KNOW IT FROM: PORK PIES, GALA PIES, AND STURDY PASTIES

This pastry has to be used straightaway, so make sure you're ready to get going with the filling of your chosen bake. For example, if you're making pork pies (see page 148), have the filling ready first. My nana taught me how to make it, using a recipe that her Lancastrian mother passed on to her. It's old school, unapologetically filling, and doesn't mess around.

KIT LIST
hand whisk

Ingredients
⅓ cup lard
½ stick unsalted butter, plus extra for greasing
¼ cup water
3 tablespoons milk
3¼ cups all-purpose flour
¾ cup strong white bread flour, plus extra for dusting
1 teaspoon salt

1 Put the lard, butter, measured water, and milk into a medium saucepan over medium heat and stir occasionally until the butter and lard have melted.

2 Mix the flours and salt together in a large bowl with a hand whisk, then pour in the hot mixture and stir to combine. Bring the mixture together with your hands to form a dough in the bowl.

3 Lightly flour a work surface, turn the dough out onto it, and **knead** for a minute or so. You need to shape this pastry as soon as you can, before it loses its heat and starts to set.

This pastry is super easy to make, but if you let it cool before molding into shape, it's like trying to work with carpet underlay. As soon as it's cool enough to touch, get involved.

This cannot be stored—use immediately.

Choux Pastry

Not as fancy as it sounds, this is a recipe that—if you get it right—is really adaptable. You could even end up building a croquembouche if you had the time or inclination. Choux is basically just a vehicle for getting as much filling into your mouth as possible in one bite.

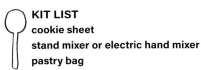

KIT LIST
cookie sheet
stand mixer or electric hand mixer
pastry bag

Ingredients
⅔ stick unsalted butter
large pinch of salt
pinch of superfine sugar
¾ cup water
½ cup all-purpose flour, sifted
⅓ cup strong white bread flour, sifted
3 eggs, beaten

Can be stored in the pastry bag in the fridge for up to 2 hours. Bring up to room temperature before piping.

1 Bring the butter, salt, sugar, and measured water to a boil in a medium saucepan, stirring to encourage the butter to melt. Remove from the heat and **shoot the flours** in, stirring vigorously to make a thick paste. Return to low heat and stir, flattening the now doughlike mixture, scraping it off the pan and stirring it again. Basically, just keep it moving because you are trying to **cook out** the flours without burning the mixture. Continue beating for about 5 minutes and then remove from the heat.

2 Spread the mixture out thinly on a lined cookie sheet to cool it as quickly as possible. When it's cold, scrape it into the bowl of a stand mixer and start to beat it (or use a bowl and an electric hand whisk). Add the beaten egg a little at a time, beating constantly. YOU MIGHT NOT NEED ALL THE EGG, so don't go throwing it all in. After the first bit of egg has been incorporated into the mixture and you can't see it any more, add a little more. You are looking for the mixture to reach **dropping consistency**.

3 Transfer to a pastry bag and use for your chosen recipe.

This is a "pastry" that will improve with practice. Maybe it won't rise the first time (perhaps your mixture was too wet). Maybe it will taste a little eggy (perhaps it needed to be cooked a little longer). If that happens, you'll know what to change for next time.

Semi Rough Puff Pastry

If you're an impatient person, please buy your puff pastry from a store, in a block or ready rolled. I've done what I can to make this simpler (hence, semi), so you won't have to do crazy things like roll out rectangles of butter, but it is still a bit of a process. Commit to it and you'll end up with a delicious flaky pastry that can be used for sweet or savory bakes, depending on your filling. And remember, the key thing is to keep everything—your equipment, the room, and even your hands—as cold as possible. Don't overwork the dough.

KIT LIST
food processor (optional)
pastry brush

Ingredients
3¾ cups all-purpose flour, plus extra for dusting
4 sticks unsalted butter, chilled and cubed
1 teaspoon salt
scant 1 cup ice-cold water

1 Put the flour, half of the butter, and the salt in a food processor and blitz briefly until the mixture looks like breadcrumbs. Add the remaining butter and, with the processor on, trickle the measured ice-cold water in very gradually. As soon as you see big clumps form, STOP blitzing. You may not need all the water. To make by hand, mix the flour and salt together in a large bowl, add half of the butter, in cubes, and rub in with your fingertips until the mixture looks like breadcrumbs, then coarsely grate in the remaining butter and stir briefly to combine. Trickle in the water very gradually while stirring until you have added just enough for big clumps to form.

2 Turn the mixture out onto a work surface, bring together with your hands to form a dough, and shape into a ball. Flatten slightly, seal in plastic wrap, and let rest in the fridge for an hour.

3 Flour a work surface. Unwrap the dough and use a rolling pin to roll out into a long rectangle with one short edge facing you. Fold the bottom third up to the middle (use a pastry brush to brush off any excess flour as you go) and then fold the top third over the bottom third. Turn the block 90 degrees and then roll out into another long rectangle again with one short edge facing you. Fold into thirds again, seal in plastic wrap, and return to the fridge for 30 minutes. This is the first stage of **lamination**.

4 Repeat this whole rolling, folding, and resting in the fridge process twice more. After the final 30 minutes of chilling, the pastry will be ready to use.

Store in the fridge until ready to use, for up to 3 days.

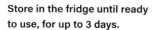

Don't have a rolling pin? Use a wine bottle. You can even put ice inside the bottle to help keep everything cold as you roll.

Grapefruit Puffs

WHO DOESN'T WANT A BIT-TER CARAMEL IN THE MORNING?

Considering this is a pretty straightforward recipe (I'm actively encouraging you to use store-bought pastry here), these puffs went through one of the most rigorous testing processes in the book. Really, I'd like to eat tarte Tatin for breakfast, but to make that more acceptable I've subbed in some grapefruit instead. The caramel balances out the bitterness of the fruit and is an opportunity to use up leftover caramel sauce, which I always seem to have lying around.

KIT LIST
cookie sheet

Ingredients
1 sheet of store-bought ready-rolled
   puff pastry
2 grapefruit, whatever color you can get
leftover caramel sauce (see Toffee Apple
   Crumble Cake on pages 72–3 or
   Banoffee Mess on page 206)—you can
   make a fresh batch of caramel sauce,
   but you need it to be cold and set when
   you spread it on the pastry
powdered sugar for water icing, to decorate
   (optional)

1 Preheat the oven to 400°F and line a cookie sheet with parchment paper. Use parchment paper here even if you normally use a silicone mat because I have found it helps to avoid a greasy, soggy bottom.

2 Unroll the pastry and cut 4 squares out of it (this will leave you with enough for another 2 squares to do whatever you like with). Score a ½-inch border within the edges of each square. Place on the lined cookie sheet and bake for 10 minutes.

3 Meanwhile, slice off the ends of each grapefruit and use a sharp knife to slice away the peel and pith. Hold the now juicy, naked grapefruit in your hand and follow the line of the natural segments with your knife to slice them into a bowl. Make sure you cut in between the membranes here so that you end up with segments free from any bitter white bits.

4 Remove the puffs from the oven and gently use your fingers to push down the central section, leaving the ½-inch border walls standing. Spread some caramel over the now indented square (I use about 1 tablespoon per puff). Arrange the grapefruit segments on top, and bake for another 10 minutes, or until golden brown.

5 Remove from the oven and transfer the puffs to a wire rack. If you want a little more sauce, heat the caramel in the microwave until it is a drizzling consistency, then pour it on top of the puffs. Alternatively, you could decorate with water icing (made using equal quantities of powdered sugar and water mixed together until smooth) for a more store-bought pastry look.

 Do not store—eat the same day.

Difficulty:

Little Maple Pecan Pies

I DEFY YOU TO EAT FEWER THAN THREE

**I found out recently that there are breadcrumbs in treacle tarts.
Shocking revelation. These little pies have a bit of the treacle tart
about them, combined with a lot of nuttiness and a lot of maple
syrup. They're bite-sized, so make sure you load up your plate.**

KIT LIST
food processor
pastry brush
12-hole muffin pan
round cookie cutter a bit larger than the muffin
    pan holes—I use a 3¼-inch cutter
stand mixer or electric hand mixer
12 paper baking cups
pie weights or dried lentils or rice for blind baking

Ingredients
3 tablespoons unsalted butter, melted, plus extra
    for greasing
all-purpose flour, for dusting
½ batch of Sweet Shortcrust Pastry (pie dough, see
    page 124) or 11 ounces ready-rolled, store-bought
    pie dough
⅓ cup lightly packed soft light brown sugar
½ cup maple syrup
3½ tablespoons light corn syrup
1 teaspoon vanilla extract
2 eggs
large pinch of salt
1 cup breadcrumbs (white bread works best, freshly
    blitzed in a food processor)
⅔ cup chopped pecans
whipped cream, to serve

WAIT, THERE'S MORE...

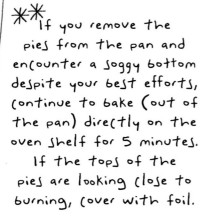

*The thinner you get the pastry, the more filling you get in your pies.

**If you remove the pies from the pan and encounter a soggy bottom despite your best efforts, continue to bake (out of the pan) directly on the oven shelf for 5 minutes.
If the tops of the pies are looking close to burning, cover with foil.

1 Brush the holes of the muffin pan with a little melted butter, making sure to reach down in the bottom of each hole. Sprinkle a little flour into the holes, then tap and rotate the pan to ensure each hole is lightly coated all the way up in flour.

2 Lightly flour a work surface and roll out the dough to a thickness of about ⅛ inch*. Use a cookie cutter to stamp out 12 circles a little larger than the holes of your muffin pan.

3 Press a dough circle into each hole of the pan, then work the dough with your thumbs up the sides until you have a small lip of dough sticking out the top of each hole. Let rest in the fridge for 30 minutes.

4 Meanwhile, preheat the oven to 400°F. Whisk together the sugar, syrups, vanilla extract, melted butter, eggs, and salt in a stand mixer or in a bowl with an electric hand mixer. Add the breadcrumbs and the chopped pecans and stir well.

5 Remove the dough-lined muffin pan from the fridge and place a paper baking cup in each hole. Fill each cup with pie weights or lentils or rice and bake for 10 minutes (this is **blind baking**). Remove the baking cups and weights (be careful, as they will be WARM), then bake for another 5 minutes. This is to ensure there are no soggy bottoms.

6 Remove from the oven, then put 2 tablespoons of the syrup mixture into each little pie shell. Bake for 8 minutes, or until the filling has puffed up and is golden brown.

7 Remove from the oven and let cool in the pan before tipping out and serving with a dollop of whipped cream.**

Store in an airtight container at room temperature for up to 4 days.

Difficulty: 🥚🥚🥚

Brart vs. Townie

WELL, WHAT WOULD YOU CALL A BROWNIE CROSSED WITH A TART?

This is the perfect cross between a tart and a brownie. There are three elements to this recipe: pastry, brownie, and ganache. Three solid skills.

KIT LIST
8- to 9-inch loose-bottomed fluted pie pan
stand mixer or electric hand mixer
rubber spatula (optional)
pie weights or dried lentils or rice for blind baking

Ingredients
all-purpose flour, for dusting
1 batch of Sweet Shortcrust Pastry (pie dough, see page 124)
2 tablespoons raspberry jam

For the brownie filling
10 ounces dark (semi-sweet) chocolate (54% cocoa solids minimum), broken into pieces
1 stick unsalted butter
½ cup superfine sugar
⅓ cup firmly packed soft light brown sugar
2 eggs
1 cup all-purpose flour
⅔ cup fresh raspberries, broken up by hand, plus extra to serve

For the ganache
1 cup heavy cream, plus extra to serve
10½ ounces milk chocolate
couple drops raspberry extract
1 tablespoon Chambord

WAIT, THERE'S MORE... ➡️

※

Don't worry if your pie dough is ripping and there are holes when you place it in the pan. Just use bits of leftover or overhanging dough to cover them up. It doesn't matter how it looks (unless you're planning on serving it upside down). Just make sure you do this before putting it into the fridge.

1 Lightly flour a work surface and roll out the dough to a thickness of about ⅛ inch. Gently lift the dough and transfer to the pie pan. Push into the base and sides using your knuckle. Leave any overhang for the time being and let rest in the fridge for at least 30 minutes.*

2 Meanwhile, make the brownie filling. Melt the dark chocolate and butter in a saucepan over low heat, stirring until smooth. Put both the sugars into the bowl of a stand mixer or a large bowl and add the chocolate mixture. Whisk on a fast speed for about 3 minutes until the mixture is lukewarm. Add the eggs one at a time, beating well after each addition. Carefully **fold** in the flour and the raspberries, then set aside.

3 Preheat the oven to 400°F. Remove the dough-lined pan from the fridge, line with foil, and fill with pie weights or dried lentils or rice. **Blind bake** for 12 to 15 minutes, then remove the foil and weights and bake for another 8 to 10 minutes until the piecrust is golden brown.

4 Spread the raspberry jam all over the bottom of the piecrust. Then pour in the brownie mixture and bake for 20 minutes until the brownie is set but still with a slight wobble. Remove from the oven and let cool completely in the pan.

5 Meanwhile, make the ganache. Heat the cream in a small saucepan over low heat until steaming but not boiling. While the cream is heating, break up the milk chocolate into small pieces and put into a bowl. Pour the hot cream over the chocolate, making sure all of it is covered, and let stand for 5 minutes to melt before stirring vigorously to form a smooth ganache. Add the raspberry extract and Chambord and stir again.

6 Once the brownie is cool, pour the ganache over the top, and place it in the fridge for an hour to set.

7 Remove from the pie pan, top with extra raspberries, and bring to room temperature before serving with cream.

 Store in the fridge for up to 2 days.

Difficulty:

Banana & Coffee Millefeuille

SLICE UP YOUR LIFE

A millefeuille is also known as a custard slice (or vanilla slice), but I wanted to impress you. Making custard can be a bit of a faff, but it's worth doing here to get these flavors right. And there's a bit of caramelizing, which is always a laugh. Assembly is important for these, but don't be disappointed when they fall apart at first bite. All good things must come to an end.

KIT LIST
hand whisk
2 large pastry bags and (optional) decorative tips
large cookie sheet
spare cookie sheet or other heavy rectangular heatproof item, for weighing down the pastry while you bake it

Ingredients
all-purpose flour, for dusting, if using homemade pastry
1 batch of Semi Rough Puff Pastry (see page 129) or 2 sheets of store-bought ready-rolled puff pastry
¼ cup superfine sugar, plus extra for sprinkling

For the banana custard
5 egg yolks
¼ cup superfine sugar
⅓ cup cornstarch
1 ripe banana, mashed
1¼ cups milk
1 cup heavy cream
¾ stick unsalted butter, softened

For the coffee custard
5 egg yolks
⅓ cup superfine sugar
⅓ cup cornstarch
1¼ cups milk
1 cup heavy cream
2 tablespoons instant coffee
¾ stick unsalted butter, softened
1 teaspoon vanilla bean paste

For the caramelized bananas
2 ripe bananas
walnut-sized lump of unsalted butter
2 to 3 tablespoons superfine sugar

1 For the banana custard, whisk the egg yolks, sugar, cornstarch, and mashed banana together in a bowl with a hand whisk until you have a pale paste. Heat the milk and cream in a medium saucepan over low heat, stirring, until steaming but not boiling. Pour a little of the hot milk mixture onto the egg yolk mixture and whisk vigorously to combine. Add the egg yolk mixture to the pan, increase the heat gradually, and stir constantly until the mixture thickens and starts to boil (it should coat the back of a spoon, and when you draw a line with your finger on the spoon it stays visible). Boil for 2 minutes to **cook out** the flour, continuing to stir. Pour into a strainer over a bowl. Press the custard through the strainer, then whisk in the butter until it melts. Cover the custard's surface with plastic wrap to stop a skin from forming.* ➞ ⟶

2 For the coffee custard, it is the same process as step 1, above, but add the instant coffee to the milk and cream while heating, stirring until dissolved, and whisk the vanilla paste into the strained custard along with the butter.

3 Transfer your cooled custards to 2 large pastry bags (fitted with pretty tips if you're so inclined—I'm not) and let rest in the fridge for at least 40 minutes.

4 Meanwhile, preheat the oven to 410°F. If using your own pastry, lightly flour a work surface, halve the pastry, and roll out one half to the length of your largest cookie sheet. Line the cookie sheet with parchment paper and transfer the pastry onto it. Sprinkle with 1 tablespoon superfine sugar, and then cover with a second piece of parchment paper. Place a second cookie sheet or alternative on top of the paper and pastry, and transfer the whole thing to the oven to bake for 15 minutes. Remove the top cookie sheet and top paper and bake for another 5 minutes. Lift the pastry from the oven and off the paper, and let cool on a wire rack until ready to use. Repeat with the remaining half of the pastry. If using store-bought pastry, just unroll each sheet in turn on your work surface and follow the same process as for the rolled-out pastry.

5 While your pastry is cooling, make the caramelized bananas. Peel the bananas and slice into rounds ⅛-inch thick. Heat a large skillet over medium heat and add the butter. Place the banana slices in the skillet, sprinkle in the superfine sugar, and fry for about 8 minutes. Flip them over and fry for another 8 minutes. The time it takes to caramelize your bananas will depend on a few factors: the water content of your bananas/whether or not your heat is fluctuating/what sort of pan you are using etc., etc., so just keep an eye on them and make the call to remove from the heat when you think they are ready. Let cool in the pan and they should start to harden up.

6 Trim any burned edges from your pastry and divide each rectangle into 12 evenly sized rectangles (so you'll have 24 in total). **Pipe** the custards alternately in 2 rows on the first rectangle and then top with a few bits of caramelized banana. Top this with a second pastry rectangle. Repeat the piping on this layer and top with banana again. Repeat this entire process until you have 8 two-tiered millefeuille.

7. Mix the powdered sugar with a drop of water and stir to remove any lumps. You are looking for a loose icing but one that will sit on the top of your final pastry rectangle without dripping off, so add the water a drop at a time. (As a wise woman once said to me: "You can always add more water but you cannot take it away.") Pour the icing across the remaining 8 pastry rectangles in a thin layer, spreading where needed, and then place each one on top of the stacks you already have.

✳ If your custard splits (and you'll know because it won't look smooth but squiggly and rank, with the fat oozing out), return it to the heat, add a splash of milk, and whisk quickly until it looks like custard again. This fix should work if you implement it before you've strained the mixture and stirred in the butter, or at post-butter stage.

 Store in the fridge if you have to, but the pastry will get soggy.

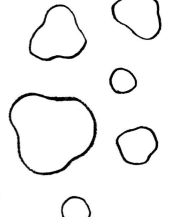

Rock & Profiterole

BLACK FOREST GATEAU STYLE

Black Forest gateau is my absolute favorite, so I took those flavors—cherry, chocolate, and cream—piped them into choux buns, and called them profiteroles. Doing the filling is tricky, but it's worth sticking with because you'll end up with a beautiful pile of deliciousness. Real rock and roll.

KIT LIST
cookie sheet
3 pastry bags
toothpick
blender or food processor
hand whisk
baking pan
electric hand mixer
rubber spatula (optional)
small plain tip

For the profiteroles
1 batch of Choux Pastry (see page 126)

For the cherry compote
15-ounce can cherries in syrup
2 tablespoons kirsch or cherry brandy
1 tablespoon cherry jam

For the crème diplomat
3 egg yolks
¼ cup superfine sugar
2 tablespoons cornstarch
1 cup milk
1 tablespoon vanilla bean paste
1 cup heavy cream

For the ganache
½ cup heavy cream
7 ounces dark (semi-sweet) chocolate (54% cocoa solids minimum)
chocolate-dipped cherries, to decorate (optional)

To make the profiteroles

1 Preheat the oven to 350°F and line a cookie sheet with parchment paper.

2 Transfer the choux to a pastry bag and snip off the tip, making a cut about ½ inch in length, depending on how large you want your choux buns to be. **Pipe** blobs (I go for the size of a ping-pong ball) onto the lined cookie sheet, leaving a 2-inch gap in between.

3 Dip your finger in a little water and stroke down the inevitable nipple on top of the buns to stop them from burning in the oven, then bake for 30 minutes.

4 Turn the buns over and pierce each one with a toothpick, then bake, hole-side up, for another 5 minutes. This lets the steam escape and stops them from getting soggy. Remove from the oven and let cool on a wire rack.*

* Now that you've mastered profiteroles, why not try my savory version on page 151?

To make the cherry compote

5 Pour the cherries, including their syrup, into a small saucepan, bring to a gentle boil, and cook until the syrup is **reduced** by half. Add the kirsch or cherry brandy and return to a simmer. After a minute or so, stir in the jam, remove from the heat, and let cool.

6 Pour into a blender or food processor and blitz to a jamlike consistency. If the compote still feels a little too runny, return it to the pan to reduce further before setting aside to cool again.

7 Transfer to a small pastry bag and set aside.

To make the crème diplomat

8 Whisk the egg yolks, sugar, and cornstarch together in a large bowl with a hand whisk until you have a pale paste. Heat the milk in a medium saucepan over low heat until steaming but not boiling. Add the vanilla paste and stir to combine. Pour half of the hot milk onto the egg yolk mixture and whisk vigorously to combine, then gradually add the remaining hot milk in a thin stream, whisking constantly until it is all incorporated. Add the egg yolk mixture to the pan, place over medium heat, and bring to a boil, whisking constantly until thickened (it should coat the back of a spoon, and when you draw a line with your finger on the spoon it stays visible). Transfer to a baking pan and spread out evenly to cool, covering with plastic wrap that is loose enough for you to press it down across the entire surface of the custard to stop a skin from forming.

9 Once cool, plop this custard (you have made a crème pâtissière—congrats!) into a bowl and whisk with a hand whisk to bring back to a smooth consistency. In a separate bowl, whip the cream with an electric hand mixer to **soft peaks** and then **fold** this into the crème pat. (The addition of the whipped cream is what turns crème pâtissière into crème diplomat—another fact for the pub quiz.)

10 Once evenly combined, transfer the crème diplomat** to a pastry bag fitted with the tip and set aside.

To make the ganache

11 Heat the cream in a small saucepan over low heat until steaming but not boiling. While the cream is heating, break up the chocolate into small pieces and put into a large bowl. Pour the hot cream over the chocolate, making sure all of it is covered, and let stand for 5 minutes to melt before stirring vigorously until smooth. Ganache made.

To assemble

12 Snip off the tip of the compote pastry bag and **pipe** a little into the hole of each bun.

13 Fill the remaining void in the buns with the crème diplomat.

14 With the holes facing upward, carefully dunk the buns in the ganache and then set them aside, chocolate-side up, on your serving plate. Top with a small splodge of compote or, if you want to get fancy, a chocolate-dipped cherry.

 Store in the fridge for up to 2 days, if you have to, but they will get soggy.

✳✳ It's important that the crème diplomat is thick enough to be piped into the profiteroles without leaking. If you don't think yours is thick enough, whip up some more heavy cream and fold half of the crème diplomat mixture into it. Keep adding what's remaining until you've got a pipeable consistency.

Difficulty:

Chocolate, Licorice & Blackcurrant Tart

A TART'S TART TART

Finding ways of getting licorice into this dessert was difficult. I don't normally like it as a flavor, but here the licorice really works as part of a rich chocolate filling, which is balanced out by tart blackcurrant. You need to prepare ahead and soak the licorice overnight so that it's soft enough to work with. This tart is probably most suitable for a grown-up dinner party dessert. Unless you know lots of children who love licorice.

KIT LIST
8- to 9-inch loose-bottomed fluted pie pan
pie weights or dried lentils or rice for
   blind baking
small food processor
metal spatula
hand whisk

For the pastry
all-purpose flour, for dusting
1 batch of Sweet Shortcrust Pastry (pie
   dough, see page 124)

To prep for the ganache

1 Put the licorice and measured warm water into a small bowl and let soften overnight.

To make the pastry

2 Lightly flour a work surface and roll out the dough to a thickness of about ⅛ inch. Gently lift and transfer it to the pie pan. Push into the base and sides using your knuckle. If the dough breaks, fear not! Use what I call the patchwork pastry method (self-explanatory) to fill in any holes, but try to keep the same thickness throughout. Don't worry about any overhang yet (we will come to it later). Rest in the fridge for 30 minutes.

3 Preheat the oven to 400°F.

4 Remove the dough-lined pie pan from the fridge, line with foil, and fill with pie weights or lentils or rice. **Blind bake** for 12 to 15 minutes. Remove the foil and weights, and bake for another 8 to 10 minutes until the bottom and sides are golden brown.

5 Remove from the oven and use a rolling pin to roll over the top of the pan—this will neatly trim any remaining overhanging piecrust for you. Let cool completely in the pan while you finish the ganache and make the blackcurrant topping.

WAIT, THERE'S MORE...

✳ If you have lumps of licorice that you don't want in your lovely smooth ganache, pass it through a strainer before it begins to cool.

For the chocolate & licorice ganache

4¼ ounces soft black licorice (this needs to be softened overnight)
½ cup warm water
1 cup heavy cream
1¼ cups milk chocolate

For the blackcurrant topping

3 cups frozen blackcurrants, plus extra to decorate
¼ cup superfine sugar
2 tablespoons lemon juice
1 tablespoon water
3 egg yolks
2 tablespoons cornstarch
3 tablespoons unsalted butter, cubed
chocolate shavings, to decorate

To finish making the ganache

6 Transfer the licorice and its soaking water to a small food processor and blitz, then scrape into a heatproof bowl. Heat the cream in a small saucepan over low heat until steaming but not boiling. While the cream is heating, break up the chocolate into small pieces and add to the bowl with the licorice. Pour the hot cream over the chocolate, making sure all of it is covered, and let stand for about 5 minutes to melt before stirring vigorously to eliminate any remaining lumps of chocolate and to incorporate the licorice.*

7 Once the piecrust is cool, pour the ganache into it, level with a metal spatula, and let set in the fridge for 2 hours.

To make the blackcurrant topping

8 Put the blackcurrants, sugar, lemon juice, and measured water into a medium saucepan over medium heat and bring to a boil. Reduce the heat and let simmer for 10 minutes until the blackcurrants start to break down. Remove from the heat and let cool slightly before blitzing in the food processor. Pass the mixture through a strainer back into the saucepan.

9 Whisk the egg yolks and cornstarch together in a small bowl with a hand whisk to make a pale paste. Add to the blackcurrant saucepan, place over low heat, and cook, stirring constantly, for about 5 minutes until thickened and it coats the back of a spoon. Add the butter and beat in until smooth and glossy.

10 Let the blackcurrant mixture cool before pouring onto the chocolate layer. Let stand in the fridge for a minimum of an hour.

11 Remove the tart from the pan and decorate with extra blackcurrants and chocolate shavings.

 Store in the fridge for up 3 days.

Difficulty:

Spring Chicken Turnovers

I FEEL MORE MUTTON DRESSED AS LAMB THESE DAYS, BUT I'LL STILL TURNOVER IF YOU ASK NICELY

Reminiscent of something you might find in your local bakery, this makes a really quick and easy supper if you've got any leftover puff pastry or store-bought sheets lying around. Make them into any shape you like—a rectangle, a triangle, a chicken. However they look, you'll end up with a delicious creamy chicken pie-type filling and some spring vegetables thrown in to make it healthy...healthy-ish.

KIT LIST
2 cookie sheets
pastry brush

Ingredients
2 sheets of store-bought ready-rolled puff
    pastry or 1 batch of Semi Rough Puff
    Pastry (see page 129)
all-purpose flour, for dusting
1 large ball of mozzarella cheese, about
    4½ ounces, thinly sliced
1 egg, beaten, for **egg wash**

For the chicken filling
oil, for frying
2 skinless free-range chicken breasts, cut
    into small pieces
2 leeks, trimmed, cleaned, and thinly sliced
1 fresh tarragon sprig, leaves picked
good glug of white wine
salt and freshly ground black pepper
¾ cup frozen peas
2 scallions, thinly sliced

For the cheese sauce
2 tablespoons unsalted butter
3½ tablespoons flour
1 cup milk
1 tablespoon whole-grain mustard
⅔ cup grated cheddar cheese

To start the chicken filling

1 Add a splash of oil to a large skillet and fry the chicken until just starting to turn opaque. Discard any liquid that comes out of the chicken. Add the leeks, tarragon leaves, and wine, and season with salt and pepper. Let simmer, stirring occasionally, while you make your cheese sauce.

To make the cheese sauce

2 Melt the butter in a medium saucepan over medium heat, add the flour, and stir until combined. Keep stirring until the mixture starts to fizz (this is the flour **cooking out**). Add the milk a tablespoon at a time, stirring vigorously. Keep adding the milk and stirring until the mixture turns from a paste to the consistency of heavy cream. Bring to a boil, stirring constantly, and boil for about 2 minutes. Remove from the heat, season with lots of pepper, and add the mustard and cheddar, stirring until the cheese has melted.

To finish the chicken filling

3 Add a generous ½ cup of cheese sauce to your chicken mixture along with the frozen peas and scallions, stir to combine, and let stand until completely cooled. You will have cheese sauce left over, so you could cook some macaroni and have mac and cheese for sustenance while dealing with the pastry.

WAIT, THERE'S MORE...

* If you start getting in a pickle and the pastry isn't playing ball, put it back in the fridge for 20 minutes and walk away. It should be easier to manipulate into the right shapes when it's colder.

4 Line 2 cookie sheets with parchment paper. If using store-bought pastry, unroll it on your work surface. If using your own pastry, lightly flour your work surface and roll out to a rectangle measuring 14 inches x 9 inches. Either way, cut the pastry into 4 equal rectangles.* Move one of these rectangles on to the top corner of one of your lined cookie sheets and spoon 3 to 4 tablespoons of the chicken mixture onto one half, leaving a ½-inch border. Top with a couple of slices of mozzarella and fold the pastry over the top of the mixture. Press down lightly with your fingers to seal the edges and then use a fork to **crimp** the edges firmly closed. Repeat with the other 3 pastry rectangles, laying them out on the cookie sheet as you go. Put this cookie sheet in the fridge while you do the same with your second piece of pastry on the other cookie sheet. Chill both sheets of pastries in the fridge for 20 minutes.

5 Meanwhile, preheat the oven to 400°F. Remove the sheets from the fridge one at a time to keep the pasties as cool as possible and brush them with the **egg wash**. Make 2 small incisions in the top of each, making sure to cut through to the mixture. Repeat with the other sheet of pastries and bake for 25 to 30 minutes until golden brown.

Store in the fridge for up to 2 days and reheat before serving.

Don't Be Scared of Pastry **147**

Difficulty:

Stick-a-Fork-in-Me Pork Pies

I'M DONE

I love pork pies but I don't like the gelatin in them; instead, I use apple to make sure they don't get too dry. I have to be honest, these are not pretty to look at, but they really do taste great. Make the filling first, because the pastry needs to be worked while it's warm, so you don't have time to muck around.

KIT LIST
pastry brush
12-hole muffin pan
2 round cookie cutters, one a bit larger than the muffin pan holes—I use a 3¼-inch cutter—and one the same size as the holes
food processor (optional)

For the filling
4¼ ounces chorizo, skinned and blitzed in a food processor or very finely chopped
½ cup grated sharp cheddar cheese
14 ounces ground pasture-raised pork
1 teaspoon dried sage
1 tablespoon whole-grain mustard
½ cooking apple, peeled, cored, and finely chopped
cracked black pepper
oil, for frying

For the pie crusts
melted butter, for greasing
all-purpose flour, for dusting
1 batch of Hot Water Crust Pastry (see page 125)
1 egg, beaten, for **egg wash**

chutney, to serve

1 First, make the filling. Mix all the ingredients apart from the oil together in a large bowl. To check the seasoning, take a little of the mixture out and fry in a little oil in a pan until browned. Taste and then season the rest of the mixture accordingly. Set aside.

2 Brush the holes of the muffin pan with a little butter, making sure to reach down into the bottom of each hole. Sprinkle a little flour into the holes, then tap and rotate the pan to ensure each hole is lightly coated all the way up in flour. This will make the cooked pies easier to remove from the pan. Trust me.

3 Preheat the oven to 400°F. Lightly flour a work surface and roll out the pastry to about ⅛ inch thick. Use a cookie cutter to stamp out 12 circles a little larger than the holes of your muffin pan.

4 Press a pastry circle into each hole of the pan, then work the pastry with your thumbs up the sides until you have a small lip of pastry sticking out the top of each hole.*

5 While the pastry is still warm, roll out again. Use a slightly smaller cutter to stamp out 12 circles for your pie lids. Set aside.

6 Fill each pastry shell with the filling and tightly pack it in. Place your lids on top of the meat mixture and then fold the pastry lip over the lid and seal as tightly as you can by squishing the pastry together. Brush with **egg wash**, then use a sharp knife to cut a small cross in the top of each pie to let the steam escape in the oven. Bake for 35 to 40 minutes until golden brown.

7 These should just fall out of your buttered and floured pan, but if not, take a sharp knife and cut around the edges, freeing them from the pan and allowing them to fall directly into your mouth.

 Store in the fridge for up to 3 days.

✳ If your pastry has become too cold, now is when you'll know it because this step will feel impossible. You can keep going, using the warmth of your thumbs to encourage the pastry up the sides, but don't worry if you end up having to make do with shallower pies.

Difficulty:

Choux Shells with Steak & Horseradish

SHE SELLS CHOUX SHELLS BY THE SEASHORE

One of the main reasons I created this was because I like saying "choux shells." A traditional British "Sunday roast dinner" often consists of a Yorkshire pudding, some beef, and a bit of horseradish, so I've replaced the Yorkshire with a choux shell to give you a canapé-sized equivalent. You could also size them up to turn them into a dinner party appetizer, and even chuck some gravy on there too. Because what isn't better with a bit of gravy?

KIT LIST
cookie sheet
2 pastry bags
toothpick
stand mixer or electric hand mixer
griddle pan (optional)

Ingredients
1 batch of Choux Pastry (see page 126)
⅔ cup heavy cream
⅔ cup cream cheese
⅓ cup horseradish sauce
2 steaks—any cut of steak you like, but filet
   mignon is best
walnut-sized lump of butter
dash of oil
salt and freshly ground black pepper
chives, chopped (optional), to garnish

1 To make the choux shells (also known as profiteroles), follow steps 1 to 4 on page 140.

2 Whip the cream and cream cheese together in a stand mixer or in a bowl with an electric hand mixer until smooth and stiff enough to **pipe**. Mix in the horseradish and season to taste with salt and pepper. Transfer to a pastry bag.

3 Fry the steak in a very hot skillet or ridged grill pan to your preference using the butter and oil, **basting** constantly. Let the steak rest for 5 minutes before thinly slicing and cutting into bite-sized pieces.

4 Slice the tops off the choux shells, snip the tip off the pastry bag, and pipe in the cream.* Top with as many slices of the steak as you like. You can also scatter them with some chopped chives to make them look a little bit green and healthy.

✱ If your choux shells end up wonky, or holey, or you can't tell the top from the bottom, just do what you can with the knife to make whatever receptacle possible to hold the cream and steak. Piped filling looks better for a party, but no judgment here of anyone wanting to dip or spread instead.

These do not store well, so eat sooner rather than later.

Difficulty:

Toad-in-the-Hole Pasties

HOW MANY DO I HAVE TO EAT BEFORE I FIND MY PRINCE?

You might have seen me make these before, but I haven't been able to share the recipe until now. So this is the moment I'm sure you've all been waiting for. I wanted to fill a pasty with the feeling of a delicious, warm, cozy dinner. Complete with mashed potatoes and gravy.

KIT LIST
baking pan
mortar and pestle (optional)
large pastry bag
cookie sheet
pastry brush
electric hand mixer (optional)

Ingredients
8 sausages
2 sheets of store-bought ready-rolled
    puff pastry or 1 batch of Semi Rough
    Puff Pastry (see page 129)
1 egg, beaten, for **egg wash**

For the red onion gravy
2 tablespoons unsalted butter, plus
    a knob for the mashed potatoes
2 or 3 red onions depending on size,
    halved and thinly sliced
1 teaspoon soft light brown sugar
1 teaspoon dried sage
1 teaspoon mustard powder
1 teaspoon fennel seeds, crushed in a
    mortar and pestle (or just on a cutting
    board using something weighty)
1 tablespoon all-purpose flour, plus extra
    for dusting if using homemade pastry
½ cup red wine—any you have on hand
1 cup beef stock
salt and freshly ground black pepper

1 Preheat the oven to 425°F and line a baking pan with foil.

2 Put the sausages into the lined pan and roast for 35 minutes, turning occasionally.

3 Meanwhile, make the red onion gravy. Melt the butter in a large skillet, add the onions with a large pinch of salt, and fry over low heat for 10 minutes, stirring occasionally. Add the sugar and fry for another 5 minutes. Next, add the sage, mustard, fennel seeds, and flour and fry for another couple of minutes, then stir in the wine and stock. Bring to a simmer and **reduce** by one-quarter, then season with salt and pepper. Let cool.

4 While your gravy is cooking, make the mashed potatoes. Cook the potatoes in a saucepan of boiling water for 15 minutes, or until soft. Drain in a colander and return to the pan. Add a knob of butter (I don't want any questions about how big a "knob" is; it is as big as you want it to be) and mash until smooth.* Season well with salt and pepper and a grating of nutmeg, if you like. Let cool and then transfer to a large pastry bag.

*If you are struggling to get the potatoes to mash smoothly, use an electric hand mixer to whip it up. Don't overdo it though or the mash will turn watery.

WAIT, THERE'S MORE...

For the mashed potatoes
2 large potatoes, such as Yukon Gold,
  peeled and cut into ½-inch slices
freshly grated nutmeg (optional)

5 Once the sausages are done, remove from the oven and let cool. Reduce the oven to 400°F.

6 Line a cookie sheet with parchment paper. If using store-bought pastry, unroll it on your work surface and cut around a small plate to cut out 3 or 4 circles from each sheet. If using your own pastry, lightly flour your work surface and roll out to a thickness of about ⅟₁₆ inch, then cut out the circles in the same way. Put the pastry circles into the fridge to keep chilled.

7 Take one pastry circle out of the fridge and place on the lined cookie sheet. Place some of the onion gravy in the center of the circle, top with a sausage, and **pipe** some mashed potatoes across the top. The quantities here are up to you. The fuller the pasties are, the harder they will be to seal, but too little mixture and you'll be serving plain pastry.

8 Once filled, brush one-half of the pastry circle rim with **egg wash** and fold the pastry in half, sealing as you go. Here you can **crimp** however you like, as long as it is tightly sealing the filling inside. I like to have 3 or 4 pasties in the oven at once, depending on their size, so once crimped, I put each pasty in the fridge until I have enough to put a batch in the oven.

9 Brush the pasties all over with egg wash. Bake for 35 minutes, or until puffed up and golden brown.

Eat immediately.

Difficulty:

Homely Homity Pies

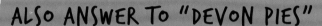

ALSO ANSWER TO "DEVON PIES"

I was brought up vegetarian, so these were a childhood staple for me. You can make them any size you like—a big pie works just as well as the little ones. They're a handy meat-free alternative at summer picnics and barbecues, and are so good that nonveggies will probably get stuck in too. Though from my days as a vegetarian, I do remember that nobody likes the meat-eater who eats all of the veggie options, so don't be that person.

KIT LIST
food processor (optional)
8 mini pie pans
cookie sheet

For the pastry*
1⅔ cups all-purpose flour, plus extra for dusting
⅔ cup whole-wheat flour
1½ sticks unsalted butter, chilled and cubed
1 teaspoon mustard powder
pinch of salt
pinch of cracked black pepper (that's a couple of twists of a grinder)
3 egg yolks
1 to 2 teaspoons ice-cold water

For the filling
walnut-sized lump of butter
¾ pound red onions, thinly sliced
4 garlic cloves, crushed
a few thyme sprigs, leaves picked
3 tablespoons white wine
¾ pound potatoes, peeled and cut into ½-inch cubes
1 tablespoon wholegrain mustard
½ cup heavy cream
1¼ cups grated sharp cheddar cheese
salt and freshly ground black pepper

This shortcrust pastry (pie dough) is made with whole-wheat flour, which I think gives the pies a healthier vibe, and mustard powder, for added flavor. You can use straight-up regular pie dough if you'd rather (see page 124).

WAIT, THERE'S MORE...

1 To make the pie dough, put the flours, butter, mustard powder, salt, and pepper into a food processor and blitz until the mixture looks like breadcrumbs. Add the egg yolks one at a time, pulsing after each addition. If making by hand, put the flours, mustard powder, salt, and pepper into a bowl, add the butter, and rub in with your fingertips until the mixture looks like breadcrumbs. Beat the egg yolks together, then gradually mix in.

2 Lightly flour a work surface. If you have a doughlike consistency (squish it between your fingers to see if it is wet enough), then turn the mixture out onto the floured surface and bring together into a ball. If, however, your mixture is still a little crumbly, add 1 teaspoon of ice-cold water and pulse or mix again. You might need to add another teaspoon of water, as this is a crumbly piecrust because of the whole-wheat flour. Seal your ball of dough tightly in plastic wrap and let rest in the fridge for 30 minutes before using.

3 Meanwhile, make the filling. Melt the butter in a large saucepan and add the onions, cover with a lid, and cook over low heat for 10 minutes, stirring occasionally. Add the garlic and cook for another 3 minutes. When the onions are becoming sticky, add the thyme, wine, and potatoes. Replace the lid and cook for another 10 minutes. This mixture will stick to the bottom of the pan, so keep checking in on it and stirring. Add the mustard, cream, and ¾ cup of the grated cheddar and stir well. Season with salt and pepper, and then set aside.

4 Preheat the oven to 400°F. Take the pie dough out of the fridge and divide into 4 evenly sized pieces. Lightly flour your work surface and roll out the first piece of dough to a thickness of about ⅛ inch.* Pick it up and place it in the first mini pie pan, using your knuckle to push it into the corners (I know circles don't have corners, but you know what I mean). Use your rolling pin to roll over the top of the pan, which will trim the dough for you. Fill any gaps you might have in the dough with offcuts and press them in so that you have an even thickness. Use a fork to prick the bottom to stop it from puffing up in the oven. Ball up the rest of the offcuts, then repeat the procedure to line all 8 mini pie pans with dough. Place them on a cookie sheet and bake for 10 minutes.

5 Remove the dough-lined mini pie pans from the oven, then fill each one to the brim with the filling mixture and top off with the remaining grated cheddar. Bake for another 25 to 30 minutes, or until the cheese is golden brown. Remove from the oven and let the pies cool before removing them from the pans.

✳ If the dough comes out of the fridge just too crumbly to work with, let it reach room temperature before trying again. If it's still impossible to roll out, break off little bits with your hands, and cover the mini pie pans as best you can. Next time, you probably need to add a touch more water.

 Store in the fridge for up to 3 days.

Give Me Puddings, Not Hugs

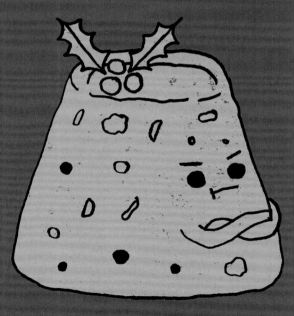

The Oxford English Dictionary suggests pudding is "a cooked sweet dish served after the main course of a meal." As far as I'm concerned, you can have pudding at whatever time of the day you like because it's a comfort food to be eaten out of a bowl, straight from the dish, off the floor—whatever works for you.

Almost all of the recipes in this chapter are designed to be a cozy treat, perfect for when you need a bit of love but don't have an alternative, like a cat. There are some old-fashioned British classics, mixed with some inventions of my own, and the best-named bake in the whole book: Plumble.

If you want to start simple, try the Wobbly Chocolate Waffle Pudding (page 162). For more of a challenge, try the Peanut Butter & Jam Roly-Poly (page 170).

Difficulty:

Ginger & Rhubarb Puddings

THINGS ARE ABOUT TO GET STEAMY

This is a small and fluffy steamed pudding. When asked to describe a steamed pudding for this introduction I replied, "It's a pudding that's steamed." I was playing it cool. I actually think they are the baking equivalent of a hug from your grandma. These are sticky with ginger and tart from the rhubarb, and need to be served straight out of the oven.

 KIT LIST
deep roasting pan with a wire rack
6 mini pudding molds or ramekins
stand mixer or electric hand mixer
rubber spatula (optional)

Ingredients
3 stalks of rhubarb
1 stick unsalted butter, plus extra for greasing
⅓ cup superfine sugar, plus 1 tablespoon for the sauce
2 eggs
2 pieces of preserved ginger, chopped
1 cup all-purpose flour, sifted with 1 teaspoon baking powder
6 tablespoons light corn syrup
6 teaspoons ginger syrup from the preserved ginger jar
1 cup water

 Not possible to store, so eat straightaway!

1 Preheat the oven to 350°F. Half-fill the roasting pan with water and set the rack into it to make a shelf for the puddings that is above the water but sits inside the pan, creating a **bain-marie**. Place in the oven, on the middle rack. Grease your mini pudding molds or ramekins.

2 Thinly slice 2 of the rhubarb stalks and line the molds from the bottom to halfway up with the rhubarb pieces.

3 Cream the butter and sugar together in a stand mixer or in a large bowl with an electric hand mixer for a couple of minutes. Add the eggs one at a time, beating well after each addition. Add the chopped ginger, **fold** in the prepared flour to make a batter, and set aside.

4 Put 1 tablespoon of light corn syrup and 1 teaspoon of ginger syrup into each mold, then divide the batter evenly between them. Place the puddings on the rack in the roasting pan above the water. Bake for 20 to 25 minutes until golden brown on top.

5 While the puddings are baking, chop the remaining rhubarb stalk, add to a small saucepan with 1 tablespoon sugar and the measured water, and simmer until mushy.

6 Remove the puddings from the oven. Place a small plate on top of each and—using a dish towel as the molds will be hot—carefully flip over. Remove the molds. Top with the stewed rhubarb to serve.*

*If these aren't served right away, it's likely they'll get stuck inside the molds, making it tricky to turn them out. So if (unlike me) you can't eat 6 puddings at once, try reheating them a little to loosen. Just pop them in the oven at 300°F for about 5 minutes. Be careful not to overbake them by leaving them in there too long.

Difficulty: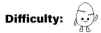

Wobbly Chocolate Waffle Pudding

SHAKE THAT THING

I really don't like bread and butter pudding. But I do like waffles and chocolate custard. That explains what we are doing here. Best served with cream or ice cream.

KIT LIST
14-inch x 10-inch baking pan or ovenproof dish
hand whisk

Ingredients
1 stick unsalted butter, softened, plus extra for greasing
2 to 3 packs of waffles for toasting, about 26 ounces in total
3½ ounces milk chocolate
3 egg yolks
¼ cup superfine sugar
1 cup milk
1 cup heavy cream, plus extra to serve (optional)
5½ ounces dark (semi-sweet) chocolate (54% cocoa solids minimum), broken into pieces
1 teaspoon vanilla bean paste
vanilla ice cream, to serve (optional)

1 Grease your baking pan or ovenproof dish liberally with butter.

2 Unpack the waffles and butter each waffle on one side. Place in the greased pan or dish butter-side up. You want the whole pan to be covered with waffles, so you may need to trim some to fit. Break up the milk chocolate and scatter the waffles with it. Butter more waffles and place them on top, again butter-side up.

3 Preheat the oven to 400°F.

4 Whisk the egg yolks and sugar together in a bowl with a hand whisk until you have a pale paste. Heat the milk, cream, dark chocolate, and vanilla paste in a medium saucepan over low heat, stirring until the chocolate has melted and the mixture is steaming but not boiling. Remove from the heat. Pour a little of this mixture onto the egg yolk mixture and whisk vigorously to combine. Add the egg yolk mixture to the pan and whisk well.

5 Pour the mixture over the waffles and bake for 30 to 35 minutes until set but still with a slight wobble.* Remove from the oven and serve immediately with cream or ice cream.

※ If the wobble is more than slight (because the pudding is runny) but the top is starting to burn, cover the dish with foil and return it to the oven.

 Store in the fridge for up to 2 days. Reheat in the microwave before serving.

Difficulty:

Little Lime & Tequila Melting Chocolate Puddings

PROBABLY SHOULDN'T OPERATE HEAVY MACHINERY AFTER CONSUMPTION

People are always banging on about how hard it is to get a chocolate fondant to melt in the middle. I guess they've never seen this recipe. No matter your skill set or your oven, a gooey melty middle is guaranteed with these instructions. The only tricky bit is turning out the puddings, unless you've got asbestos hands, in which case you'll be fine. The tequila is totally optional (though I think it gives the puddings the edge they need). Perfect after dinner; dangerous as breakfast, and that's speaking from experience.

KIT LIST
4 mini pudding molds
pastry brush
Microplane
stand mixer or electric hand mixer
rubber spatula (optional)
cookie sheet

Ingredients

1 stick unsalted butter, cubed, plus extra, melted, for greasing
unsweetened cocoa powder, for sprinkling (optional)
10 ounces dark (semi-sweet) chocolate (54% cocoa solids minimum), broken into pieces
⅓ cup firmly packed soft light brown sugar
2 eggs, plus 1 egg yolk
zest of 1 to 2 limes, depending on how strong you want the citrus kick to be, and juice of 1
3 tablespoons tequila
½ cup all-purpose flour, plus extra for sprinkling (optional)

WAIT, THERE'S MORE...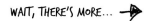

Give Me Puddings, Not Hugs **165**

The puddings can now be baked or kept in the fridge until needed (they will keep for 2 days).

1 Preheat the oven to 400°F and brush the insides of your pudding molds with melted butter (depending on your molds, you might want to add a light sprinkling of cocoa or flour on top of the butter to make it easy to tip them out when baked).

2 Melt the chocolate and butter together in a large microwave-safe bowl in the microwave using the **heat, stir, repeat** method until smooth, then let cool.

3 Whisk the sugar, whole eggs and yolk, and lime zest together in a stand mixer or in a large bowl with an electric hand mixer until well combined. Add the lime juice and tequila and whisk again. Pour in the melted chocolate mixture and whisk again. Sift in the flour, then **fold** in to combine.

4 Divide the mixture evenly between your molds and place on a cookie sheet.*

5 Bake the puddings for 10 to 12 minutes depending on how cold they are to start off with. Remove from the oven. To unmold, place a serving plate on top of each pudding in turn and flip over, then use a dish towel to grasp the hot mold and gently shake until the pudding turns out onto the plate. If they are a little stuck, try tapping the top of the molds. If all else fails, flip them back over and serve in the molds with some ice cream. No one will care, or know any different. They'll think you meant to do this all along.**

** If you've left the puddings in the molds for too long, you'll end up with a boozy chocolate cake instead of a fondant. Whip up some chocolate custard (see page 183) and serve with the puds to make up for the lack of oozy middle.

Once baked, these should be eaten straightaway.

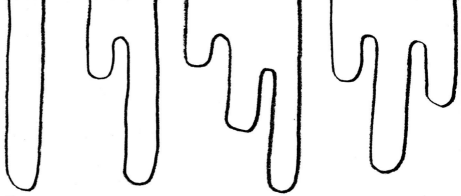

Difficulty:

Two-faced Sticky Toffee Pudding

THIS ONE'S SWEET & SOUR

A pub classic, but mine comes with a twist. This recipe uses sour cherries to create a bit of a difference, and a splash of kirsch or cherry brandy for a more grown-up flavor. So it's sweet and sour, just like that two-faced b** you knew at school. Serve warm with vanilla ice cream for full impact.**

KIT LIST
9-inch square baking pan
stand mixer or electric hand mixer
rubber spatula (optional)
food processor

Ingredients
¾ stick unsalted butter, softened, plus extra
  for greasing
½ cup lightly packed soft dark brown sugar
¼ cup superfine sugar
2 eggs, beaten
1½ cups all-purpose flour
½ teaspoon ground cinnamon
¼ teaspoon ground ginger
pinch of salt
1 cup dried cherries, chopped into small pieces

1 cup pitted, coarsely chopped dates
½ cup kirsch or cherry brandy
¾ cup hot water
1 teaspoon baking soda
vanilla ice cream, to serve

For the sauce
1 stick unsalted butter
¼ cup superfine sugar
¼ cup lightly packed soft dark brown sugar
⅔ cup heavy cream

WAIT, THERE'S MORE... ➔

1 Preheat the oven to 400°F and grease your baking pan liberally with butter.

2 Cream the butter and sugars together in a stand mixer or in a large bowl with an electric hand mixer for at least 4 minutes. Add the eggs one at a time, beating well after each addition. Sift in the flour and spices and add the salt and cherries. **Fold** into the batter.

3 Put the dates, kirsch or cherry brandy, measured hot water, and baking soda into a heatproof bowl. Set aside for 10 minutes.

4 Transfer the soaked dates to a food processor and blitz until you have a loose brown paste, being careful to avoid any hot and sticky splashes. Don't worry about any little lumps of date. Add to the batter and fold in to combine.

5 To make the sauce, put all the ingredients into a small saucepan and bring to a boil over medium heat, stirring constantly until well combined and thickened. This should take about 3 to 5 minutes.

6 Pour half of the sauce into your greased pan. Top with the batter, spreading it out evenly. Don't panic if it looks like cat vomit at this stage. The taste will make up for it. Bake for 35 minutes. If it is not cooked in the middle (insert a skewer into the center and if it comes out clean it is cooked) but is browning on the outside, cover with foil and return to the oven for 5 to 10 minutes.

7 Remove from the oven and pour the remaining sauce evenly over it*. Scoop out of the pan and serve with vanilla ice cream.

✳ If you've left the sauce while you've been eating, baking, or just living your life, it might have solidified or become grainy. You'll need to reheat it in order to pour it over the pudding, but it's important that you reheat it SLOWLY, otherwise the butter might split and it will be difficult to work with. If this does happen, add a splash of water and/or cream to get you back on track.

**Store in the fridge for up to 3 days.
Reheat in the microwave before serving.**

Difficulty:

Peanut Butter & Jam Roly-Poly

A VERY BRITISH, VERY STODGY, VERY ROLY-POLY PUDDING

This is a sickeningly sweet pudding best served with custard (see page 183). Don't shy away from the stodge. Embrace it! But make sure you throw in the fresh raspberries for the much-needed zing they add.

KIT LIST
deep roasting pan with a wire rack
hand whisk
small metal spatula (optional)
cookie sheet
pastry brush

Ingredients
1⅔ cups all-purpose flour, sifted with
    1½ teaspoons baking powder, plus
    extra flour for dusting
½ cup beef suet (vegetable suet will
    also work)
1 tablespoon superfine sugar
pinch of salt
3 tablespoons milk
2 eggs
¼ cup peanut butter (crunchy or smooth)
¼ cup jam (your favorite flavor)
⅔ cup fresh raspberries
unsalted butter, for greasing
hot custard, to serve (see page 183
    for homemade)

1 Preheat the oven to 400°F. Half-fill the roasting pan with water and then set the the rack into it to make a shelf for your pudding that is above the water but sits inside the pan, creating a **bain-marie**. Place in the oven on the middle rack.

2 Mix the prepared flour, suet, sugar, and salt together in a large bowl. In a small bowl, whisk the milk and one of the eggs together with a hand whisk. Pour into the flour mixture and stir until combined.

3 Flour a work surface, turn the mixture out onto it, and **knead** until you are confident that you can roll it out with a rolling pin.

4 Roll out into a rectangle measuring 12 inches x 8 inches. Trim off any bits you don't need.

5 Using a teaspoon or a small metal spatula, spread the peanut butter onto the dough, leaving a ½-inch border. Then spread the jam on top of the peanut butter. Tear the raspberries and dot evenly over the jam.

Store in an airtight container at room temperature for up to 2 days. Reheat to serve if you like.

✳ *If you squeeze too hard (feedback some of us might have heard before) you'll find that too much of your filling spills out of the ends. Don't unroll your pudding completely; roll it back enough to create space to pop what you can back in and keep rolling, but learn from your mistakes.*

6 Starting at one of the shorter edges, roll up the dough, applying pressure evenly and ensuring the seal is on the bottom.*

7 Grease a large piece of parchment paper liberally with butter. Gently lift the roll and place in the center of the greased paper, sealed-side down. Bring the 2 long sides together, with the roll in the middle, and fold the paper over to seal it. Do not wrap the paper too tightly around the roll as you need to allow for it to rise in the oven. Twist or fold the ends of the paper. Repeat the process with a sheet of foil and twist the ends. Place the package on the rack in the pan and bake for 50 minutes.

8 The pudding is ready to be sliced and served at this point, but I really like a crust on the outside. To achieve this, line a cookie sheet with parchment paper, then remove the pudding from the foil and paper and place it on top. Beat the remaining egg, brush it over the pudding, and bake for a final 10 minutes. Don't worry if it cracks down the middle. It still tastes good and anyway you should cover it in hot custard before serving so no one will see any imperfections.

LOOK AT THE PHOTO ➔ ➔

Lemon & Raspberry Soufflé

RISE TO ANY OCCASION

When I see recipes for soufflé, I skip straight over them. I can't handle the anxiety. Will they rise? Will I have invented a new way to scramble an egg?... etc., etc. Blah. But this recipe is different. It is a light, airy, not-too-sweet pudding that is perfect after a big meal, and I've made it so many times that I can say with confidence that it is very hard to mess up.

KIT LIST
ovenproof dish, ideally 11 inches x 9 inches
small food processor
Microplane (optional)
stand mixer or electric hand mixer
rubber spatula (optional)

Ingredients
½ stick unsalted butter, softened, plus
    extra for greasing
1¼ cups fresh raspberries, plus extra
    to serve
1 cup superfine sugar
zest of 1 lemon and 2 tablespoons juice
3 **eggs, separated**
⅔ cup heavy cream
⅓ cup milk
½ cup all-purpose flour
⅓ cup powdered sugar, for dusting

1 Preheat the oven to 350°F and grease the ovenproof dish.

2 Blitz the raspberries in a small food processor, then pass through a strainer into a bowl, discarding the seeds. Put the raspberry puree back in the processor along with the butter, sugar, and lemon zest and juice. Blitz until you have a paste. Add the egg yolks, cream, milk, and flour and blitz again.

3 Whisk the egg whites to **soft peaks** in a stand mixer or in a large bowl with an electric hand mixer. If you make the whites too stiff, they'll be harder to combine with the mixture, so don't take them too far.

4 Pour one-third of the raspberry mixture into the egg whites and gently **fold** in. Repeat with the remaining raspberry mixture until evenly distributed and well mixed.*

5 Pour the mixture into your greased dish, place it in a deep roasting pan, and transfer to the oven. Before you shut the oven door, pour some hot water into the roasting pan so that it reaches halfway up the sides of the dish to create a **bain-marie**. Bake for 40 minutes, or until lightly brown on top. Serve with raspberries and sifted with powdered sugar to take the edge off any sourness.

*If you have little white lumps of egg white showing through the mixture, fear not! Just gently whisk them out. Leaving them in isn't the end of the world, but it will result in darker brown lumps on the surface of the finished pudding.

 Not easy to store, so eat on the same day.

Difficulty:

I Hate Christmas Pudding

& CHRISTMAS

This recipe was just a title for a long time. I hate Christmas pudding and feel a bit cheated when I get passed a lump of chocolate Yule log instead, so I wanted to come up with a better alternative. At one point I thought I'd cook a whole clementine in the middle of it, but I dumped that idea because it was too hard. The point of this orangey steamed pudding is that it's got all the grown-up, comforting notes of a Christmas pudding, but it's actually nice.

KIT LIST
1 32-ounce (1-quart) ovenproof bowl
stand mixer or electric hand mixer
hand whisk
rubber spatula (optional)
string
large saucepan or Dutch oven big enough
  to fit the ovenproof bowl, with a lid

Ingredients
1½ sticks unsalted butter, softened, plus
  extra for greasing
4 or 5 satsumas or clementines, UNPEELED
  and thinly sliced into rounds, discarding
  the ends
3 tablespoons light corn syrup
1 cup lightly packed soft dark brown sugar
3 eggs
2 tablespoons Grand Marnier
2 teaspoons orange extract
1½ cups all-purpose flour sifted with
  1½ teaspoons baking powder
¼ teaspoon salt
1 teaspoon mixed spice (see page 194)
½ teaspoon ground ginger
½ teaspoon ground cinnamon
¼ teaspoon ground nutmeg
¼ cup ground almonds
1½ tablespoons good-quality marmalade
brandy cream, to serve

1 Grease the ovenproof bowl with butter. Arrange the satsuma or clementine slices to cover the inside of the bowl. Drizzle in the light corn syrup. It will pool at the bottom, which is fine.

2 Cream the butter and sugar in a stand mixer or in a large bowl with an electric hand mixer. In a small bowl, beat the eggs and Grand Marnier together with a hand whisk, then slowly add to the butter mixture, whisking constantly. Add the orange extract and whisk again. Sift in the prepared flour, salt, and spices. Add the ground almonds and **fold** in until combined. Add the marmalade and gently mix in, being careful not to knock out the air.

3 Scrape the batter into the bowl; the fruit slices should stay put, but press them against the buttery sides if they start to come loose. Take a large piece each of parchment paper and foil. Lay the parchment paper on the foil, then fold to make a pleat down the middle (this is to allow for the rise in the pudding). Place over the bowl, paper-side down, with the pleat running across the center of the bowl, and use a piece of string to secure in place just under the rim of the bowl.

4 Stand the bowl inside a large saucepan or Dutch oven. Pour boiling water into the pan until it comes one-third of the way up the sides of the bowl. If the water level is too high, there is a danger that water will get into the pudding. Cover and let simmer for 2 hours. Lifting the lid will remove the steam that you are trying so hard to create, so just listen for the bubbles of the boil to tell you when the heat is too high or too low. If the bubbling noise stops, the water has evaporated and you need to top it off ASAP. If this happens, remove the lid, pour some more water down the side, replace the lid, and bring up to a simmer again.

✳ One or more of your satsuma/clementine rounds ◄ might get left behind in the pudding bowl. Remembering that the bowl is hot, retrieve them and use a blob of light corn syrup to stick them back onto the pudding.

5 After 2 hours, remove the pan from the heat and take the bowl out of the water. This will be HOT, so use oven mitts or a dish towel. Remove the string and the foil/paper. Quickly invert onto a serving plate and gently remove the bowl.* This is now ready to serve with a brandy cream (once you've set it alight, of course)! If you want to make it ahead of a Christmas feast (because who has a burner to spare for 2 hours on Christmas Day?), it can also be microwaved to heat up before serving.

WATCH YOUR EYEBROWS... ➔ ➔

Store at room temperature for up to 5 days.

Difficulty:

Lemon & Blueberry Clafoutis

TRY SAYING THAT QUICKLY AFTER A WHISKEY

What is "clafoutis"? I tried translating it online and it means "clafoutis," so that's not helpful. But it's essentially a set custard or batter that you serve lukewarm. This is my hot pudding chapter, not my lukewarm pudding chapter, so I eat it hot (or cold). Oh, and it's super simple to make.

KIT LIST
9-inch square baking pan
Microplane (optional)
stand mixer or electric hand mixer

Ingredients
unsalted butter, for greasing
1¾ cups fresh blueberries
zest of 1 lemon
2 tablespoons kirsch or cherry brandy
3 eggs, plus 1 egg yolk
1 teaspoon almond extract
¼ cup superfine sugar
½ cup all-purpose flour
1 teaspoon baking powder
pinch of salt
⅔ cup milk
½ cup heavy cream
maple syrup, for drizzling

1 Preheat the oven to 400°F and grease your baking pan liberally with butter.

2 Scatter the blueberries across the bottom of the pan and sprinkle with the lemon zest. Pour the kirsch or cherry brandy evenly over the blueberries and set aside.

3 Whisk the whole eggs and yolk, almond extract, and sugar together in a stand mixer or in a large bowl with an electric hand mixer until light and frothy. Sift in the flour, baking powder, and salt, and whisk again until smooth. Add the milk and cream, and whisk again to combine.

4 Pour the batter on top of the blueberries (they will rise to the surface) and bake for 40 minutes. Remove from the oven and drizzle with maple syrup to taste. This is a dish best served warm, but be careful because those blueberries will be hotter than the sun when you bite down on them.

 This doesn't store very well, so eat the same day.

Difficulty:

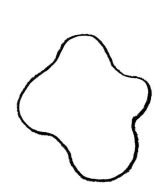

Plumble

BEST NAME IN THE BOOK

Plum Crumble. Plumble. This is super easy. It's got warm flavors. Think post-roast-beef dinner on a Sunday night or Christmas time. I'm quite proud of it. And the red wine is absolutely not optional.

KIT LIST
**ovenproof dish, ideally 11 inches x 9 inches
Microplane (optional)
food processor**

Ingredients
3 cups coarsely chopped pitted fresh plums
3 tablespoons red wine
1 tablespoon elderflower cordial
1 tablespoon water
½ teaspoon ground ginger
2 star anise
1 teaspoon vanilla bean paste
ice cream or custard (see page 183 for homemade), to serve

For the crumble
1¼ sticks unsalted butter, chilled and cubed, plus extra for greasing the dish
1⅔ cups all-purpose flour
½ cup ground almonds
⅓ cup turbinado sugar
pinch of salt
zest of 1 orange

1 Put the plums into a large saucepan with the red wine, cordial, measured water, ginger, and star anise, cover with the lid, and bring to a gentle simmer. Cook for about 10 to 15 minutes until softened but still holding their shape.

2 Meanwhile, preheat the oven to 400°F and lightly grease your oven dish with butter.

3 Remove the plums from the heat, pick out the star anise, and stir in the vanilla paste, then transfer to the greased dish.

4 Put all the ingredients for the crumble into a food processor and blitz until the mixture looks like breadcrumbs. Top the plum mixture with the crumble and bake for 30 minutes until golden brown on top.*

✳ I literally can't imagine what could go wrong with this. If you manage to mess this up, please let me know at info@lottiebedlow.com, and there might even be a prize (depending on how well this book sells).

**Store in the fridge for up to 3 days.
Reheat in the microwave before serving.**

Difficulty:

✳ For chocolate custard, break up 5½ ounces dark (semi-sweet) chocolate (54% cocoa solids minimum), add it to the pan with the milk and cream, and stir until melted.

Foolproof Custard

I PITY THE FOOL WHO CANNOT MAKE THIS CUSTARD

It's a very traditional British thing to serve a lot of the puddings in this chapter with custard, so here's how to whip up some of your own.

KIT LIST
hand whisk

Ingredients
2 egg yolks
¼ cup superfine sugar
2 teaspoons cornstarch
½ cup milk
½ cup heavy cream
1 teaspoon vanilla bean paste

1 Whisk the egg yolks, sugar, and cornstarch together in a bowl with a hand whisk until you have a pale paste. Heat the milk and cream in a medium saucepan over low heat, stirring, until steaming but not boiling.*

2 Gradually pour half of the hot milk mixture onto the egg yolk mixture in a thin stream, whisking constantly until combined. Add the egg yolk mixture to the pan and stir constantly over low heat until the mixture starts to thicken.

3 When the mixture just starts to boil, remove from the heat and stir in the vanilla paste. If you want a thicker custard, then cook it for longer, stirring constantly.

4 Your custard is ready, but to make it really smooth, pour it through a strainer over a bowl, just to get rid of any annoying bits of egg that might ruin your day.**

5 If you aren't using the custard straightaway, cover the surface with plastic wrap to stop a skin from forming. Unless you are one of those people who like the skin...

✳✳
For a boozy finish, stir in a couple tablespoons of alcohol. It will make the custard thinner, but it will taste GREAT. I can confirm this works with Baileys, Malibu, Cointreau, whiskey...

TURN OVER AND WATCH CUSTARD
THICKEN BEFORE YOUR VERY EYES... ▷ ▷

 Store in the fridge (once cooled) for up to 2 days. Reheat in the microwave before serving.

Pass It On, Please

This chapter started out as a collection of recipes inspired by childhood memories and family favorites. I then threw in a few ideas from friends for good measure. Everything in here has been passed down or given to me lovingly in one way or another. So, as I don't plan on having any children, I'm passing them on to you instead.

These are the recipes I like the most, and that I feel properly attached to. Forget about dinner party guests or impressing your coworkers with a fancy cake, these are things I just want you to enjoy eating as much as I do. So, begin the day with a Cheese Dream (page 211), have a slice of Granny June's Malt Bread (page 188) with your midmorning coffee, pop a few Scotch eggs (page 212) in your lunchbox, and then—unless you want a Gingerbread Shed (pages 193-7) for dinner—find something else in the book for your main meal before finishing the day with a bit of Banoffee Mess (page 206). Sorted.

Difficulty:

Granny June's Malt Bread

GUARANTEED TO STICK BETWEEN YOUR TEETH

Granny June used to drop off two loaves of this malt bread a week and the family would always fight over who would have the ends, or the "heel" as she would call it. It's taken a fair while to nail the recipe because I never asked her how she made it. And who would have guessed that I'd end up needing it for a recipe book that I was writing?

KIT LIST
9-inch x 5-inch x 3-inch loaf pan
pre-cut loaf pan liner (optional)
hand whisk
small angled (cranked) metal spatula
(optional)

Ingredients
1¼ cups all-purpose flour sifted with
   1 teaspoon baking powder
⅔ cup raisins
¼ cup turbinado sugar
⅓ cup malted milk powder (I use Ovaltine)
½ cup milk
1½ tablespoons light corn syrup
butter, to serve

1 Preheat the oven to 350°F and line the loaf pan with parchment paper or a pre-cut loaf pan liner.

2 Mix all the dry ingredients together in a large bowl with a hand whisk until evenly combined.

3 Heat the milk in a small saucepan until warm, add the light corn syrup, and stir to combine. Remove from the heat and pour into the dry ingredients, stirring with a spoon until combined, making sure to get rid of the pockets of flour at the bottom of the bowl.

4 Transfer to the lined loaf pan, pushing the mixture right into the corners.* Bake for 45 minutes. Remove from the oven and let cool in the pan before removing and slicing. This step is important as it continues cooking in the pan for some time, so taking it out of the pan when it is still warm will result in a loaf that is undercooked. Serve with lots of butter! You can also slice it and toast it.

* If you plop your mixture into the pan and it's refusing to nestle into the corners, try dipping a small metal spatula or the back of a teaspoon into a bit of milk and using that to spread it.

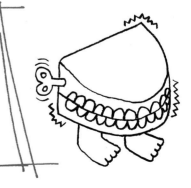

Store in an airtight container at room temperature for up to 4 days.

Difficulty:

Amelia's Cake

BUT SHE'S HAPPY TO SHARE

My friend Amelia had never baked a day in her life before signing up to help me with this book. So when I asked her to invent her own recipe for this chapter, I was incredibly proud of what she came up with. Inspired by a chocolate wafer cake her grandma used to make, and her love of hazelnut, the aim was to create a cake equivalent to all of those flavors. At one point we tried making tort wafers from scratch, but that was impossible without a waffle maker. Still, we are pleased with what we've ended up with.

KIT LIST

2 jelly roll pans or flat-bottomed baking pans
    about 9½ inches x 13½ inches
food processor
stand mixer or electric hand mixer
rubber spatula (optional)
small metal spatula
cake board (optional)
serrated bread knife
Microplane (optional)

For the cake layers

1¾ cups hazelnuts, ideally roasted but otherwise
    roast them yourself (see page 44, step 3)
2 cups powdered sugar
⅔ cup all-purpose flour
5 eggs, plus 4 egg whites
¼ cup superfine sugar
3 tablespoons unsalted butter, melted and cooled

For the ganache

⅔ cup heavy cream
8 ounces dark (semi-sweet) chocolate (54% cocoa
    solids minimum), plus extra to decorate

For the frosting

½ stick unsalted butter, softened
⅓ cup cream cheese
1½ cups powdered sugar
2 tablespoons Frangelico

WAIT, THERE'S MORE... ➡

To make the cake layers

1 Preheat the oven to 425°F and line the baking pans with parchment paper. Blitz the hazelnuts, powdered sugar, and flour together in a food processor. This makes the mixture super fine. Add the whole eggs and blitz again to make a paste.

2 Whisk the egg whites in a stand mixer or in a large bowl with an electric hand mixer until white and foamy. Add the superfine sugar 1 tablespoon at a time, beating constantly. When the final sugar is added, continue to beat for another couple of minutes. When you rub some of the mixture between your thumb and forefinger, it should feel smooth, not grainy. If it is still grainy, continue to beat until the sugar has dissolved.

3 Stir one-third of the whites into the hazelnut batter until combined, then gently **fold** in the rest of the whites. Fold in the melted butter, then transfer to the lined pans, spread out evenly with a small metal spatula, and bake for about 10 to 12 minutes. (The cake layers are supposed to be very thin, so don't panic.) Let them cool completely in the pans while you make the fillings.

To make the ganache

4 Heat the cream in a small saucepan over low heat until steaming but not boiling. While the cream is heating, break the chocolate into small pieces and place in a heatproof bowl. Pour the hot cream over the chocolate, making sure all of it is covered, and let stand for about 5 minutes to melt before stirring vigorously to form a smooth ganache. Cover the bowl with plastic wrap and let chill in the fridge for about 30 minutes to thicken and become spreadable.

To make the frosting

5 Beat the butter, cream cheese, and powdered sugar together until smooth. I find this easiest in a food processor (and it means you don't have to sift in the powdered sugar), but otherwise beat the butter and cream cheese together in your stand mixer or in a large bowl with an electric hand mixer, then sift in the powdered sugar and beat in. Don't overbeat or you will make a very runny frosting. Add the liqueur and mix for a final time. Taste, and if you want it a little stronger in flavor, add more, but just bear in mind that you will be making it thinner the more you add, which may not be easy to use when it comes to assembling the cake.

To assemble

6 Transfer one of the cake layers to a cutting board, peel off the paper, and cut widthwise into 3 equal-sized rectangles. Repeat with the second layer. Put the first of the 6 layers on a serving plate or cake board and spread a layer of ganache evenly over it.* Stack with a second layer, then spread with some of the frosting (don't be stingy—the layers of frosting are key to stopping the cake from being too dry) and stack with a third layer. Repeat the process with ganache and frosting until you have used up all the layers of cake. Pressing down on the cake, slice the sides with a serrated bread knife to make a neat rectangle. Spread the very top of cake with the remaining frosting, then grate some dark chocolate onto it. I let my cake rest in the fridge before serving to make it easier to slice.

✳ If the ganache is too thick to spread, leave it out of the fridge for a while to warm up, then beat with a hand whisk until smooth again.

 Store in the fridge for up to 2 days.

Difficulty:

Gingerbread Shed

OFFERS IN EXCESS OF £1.5M (THIS SHED IS IN LONDON)

This is the closest I'll ever come to owning property. I've never been able to make anything from gingerbread that was worthy of being called a "house," so I've scaled back my expectations to a shed. Which, in retrospect, is essentially just a smaller house. But at least it sounds less Christmassy and can be made all year round. This is a real opportunity to get creative. I've given you the right quantities and measurements here, but everything beyond the structure is up to you, so decorate it however you like. There should even be a little bit of extra dough for making some gingerbread people, or gingerbread flowerpots or a gingerbread lawn mower, etc. FYI, assembly is easier with an extra pair of hands.

KIT LIST
2 or 3 cookie sheets, ideally; if not 1 will do
hand whisk
metal spatula
plus whatever you need for decorating as
    you like, such as piping bags

Ingredients
1 cup firmly packed soft dark brown sugar
1⅓ sticks unsalted butter
¼ cup light corn syrup
4 cups all-purpose flour, plus extra for
    dusting
1½ teaspoons baking soda
3 tablespoons ground ginger
1½ teaspoons ground cinnamon
1 teaspoon mixed spice
½ teaspoon salt
a few twists of cracked black pepper
1 large egg, beaten
3 colored hard candies, for the windows
5½ ounces hard caramels (I use Werther's
    Original Caramel Hard Candies)
powdered sugar, for water icing (optional)
anything you fancy to decorate your shed,
    gum drops, cotton candy, edible moss, etc.

1 Heat the sugar, butter, and light corn syrup in a large saucepan over low heat and stir until the butter has melted. Remove from the heat and set aside.

2 Sift the flour, baking soda, spices, and salt into a large bowl. Add the cracked black pepper and stir together with a hand whisk. Pour the sugar and butter mixture into the flour mixture and stir to combine. Add the beaten egg and stir again.

3 Flour a work surface, turn the mixture out onto it, and bring together with your hands to form a dough. Once you are happy that the dough hasn't got any streaks of flour in it, seal in plastic wrap and let rest in the fridge for a minimum of an hour.

4 Preheat the oven to 400°F and line 2 or 3 cookie sheets with parchment paper. And don't worry. If you only have one, the process will just take a little longer.

5 Flour your work surface and roll out the dough to a thickness of about ⅛ inch. Create your own templates from those given on pages 195–7, and use these to cut the shed sides, roof, windows, and door from the gingerbread. I find it helpful to do this on the parchment paper, as you can then easily transfer the whole thing to your cookie sheets.

WAIT, THERE'S MORE...

* If your shed sections aren't lining up perfectly and there are spaces between the walls and in the roof, the caramel candy glue can save the day. Use the back of a teaspoon to spread it like a cement and fill any dangerous gaps.

6 Place a colored hard candy in each window hole. The candies will melt and give you a windowpane, while reinforcing the structure of that section.

7 Bake each piece for 10 to 12 minutes. Remove from the oven and let cool completely on the sheets before moving the gingerbread pieces, as they will still be soft.

8 Once all the gingerbread pieces have cooled, make the glue to stick them together. Melt the caramel candies in a large saucepan over medium heat. This is VERY sticky and VERY hot, but it saves faffing around with caramel. Throughout assembly you're going to need to play around with the heat to make sure the glue stays melted but doesn't burn. Carefully (and I mean EXTREMELY CAREFULLY) stick the sides of A, B, C, and D together (as shown on page 198). Keep holding the pieces in place until the glue sets. To attach the roof sections E and F, use a metal spatula to spread a little glue on the top edges of A, B, C, and D before pressing the roof sections gently on, one at a time, so they meet in the middle. The glue sets almost instantly, so do this as quickly as possible or it will harden on your knife.* Attach the door piece G along the side of the door hole in D (I like to have mine slightly ajar).

9 I assemble and then decorate, but there's no rule to say you couldn't decorate and then assemble. I think I just worry that if I've put loads of effort into decorating it and then it snaps when I stick it together I will be doubly sad. So **pipe** whatever you like with water icing (made using equal quantities of powdered sugar and water mixed together until smooth): hinges on the door, window frames etc., and go crazy with the candies, or keep it nice and simple. Remember, this is just a shed after all.

To make Mixed Spice
Combine together 1 tablespoon ground cinnamon, 2 teaspoons of ground coriander and 1 teaspoon each of ground nutmeg, ground ginger and ground allspice (if available), plus ½ teaspoon of ground cloves. Store the Mixed Spice in an airtight container in a cool, dry place.

 Store anywhere you can for up to 2 days.

TEMPLATES FOR YOUR GINGERBREAD SHED

A and B

Cut out 2 of these to form the ends of your shed.

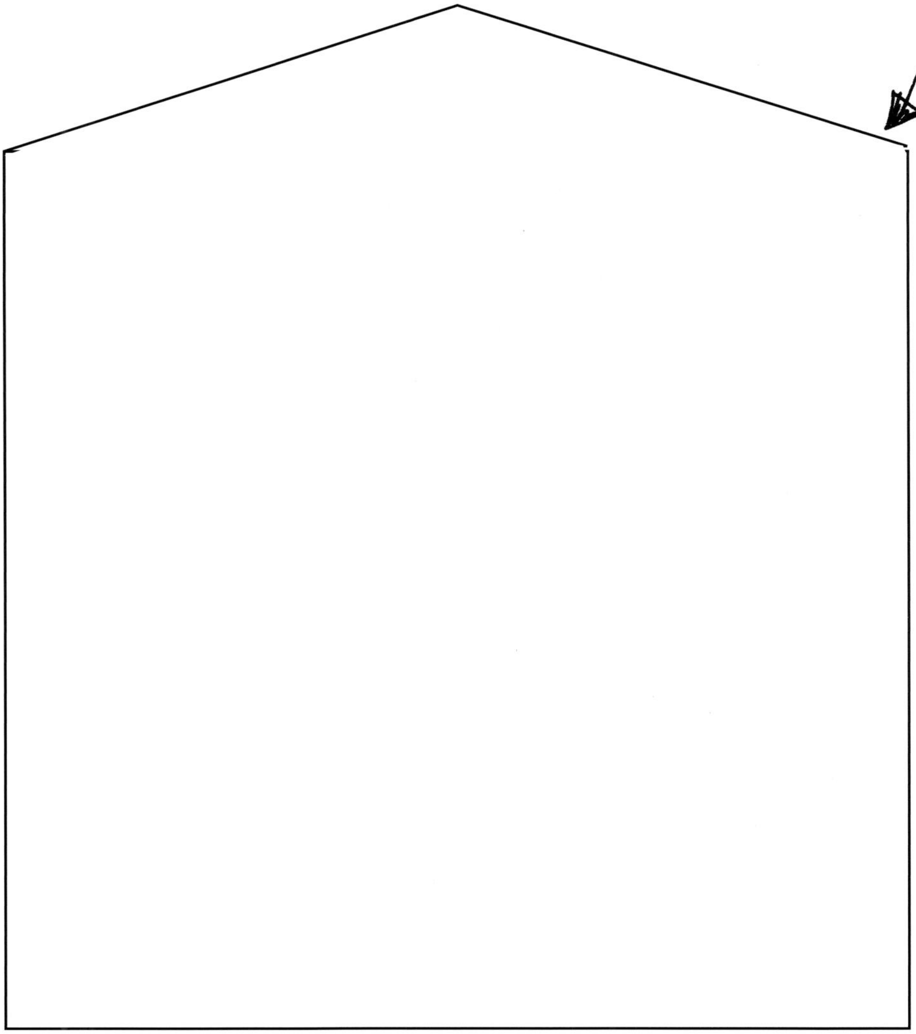

MORE TEMPLATES THIS WAY ➡

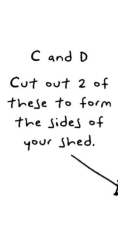

C and D

Cut out 2 of these to form the sides of your shed.

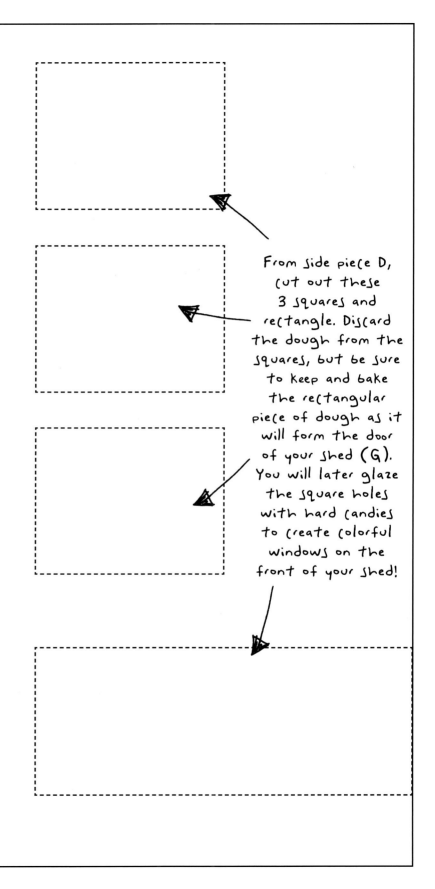

From side piece D, cut out these 3 squares and rectangle. Discard the dough from the squares, but be sure to keep and bake the rectangular piece of dough as it will form the door of your shed (G). You will later glaze the square holes with hard candies to create colorful windows on the front of your shed!

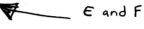

E and F

Cut out 2 of
these to form the
roof of your shed.

FINALLY TIME TO CONSTRUCT YOUR SHED...➤ ➤

Difficulty:

Nana's Bakewell Bites

NOT CERTIFIED BY THE TOWN OF BAKEWELL IN DERBYSHIRE

Before you come for me, YES I do know that this is not a traditional Bakewell tart because there is no frangipane in the recipe. But, NO, I don't care because it uses almond extract and that does the job just fine in my opinion. Nana always has batches and batches of these Bakewell bites ready to go because I said I liked them once. I even used to get them posted to me at university, so I can confirm that they do travel well.

KIT LIST
15-inch x 11-inch shallow baking pan
pie weights or dried lentils or rice for blind baking
stand mixer or electric hand mixer
hand whisk
rubber spatula (optional)
metal spatula (optional)

Ingredients
1⅔ sticks unsalted butter, softened, plus extra for greasing
1½ cups all-purpose flour sifted with 1½ teaspoons baking powder, plus extra flour for dusting
1 batch of Sweet Shortcrust Pastry (pie dough, see page 124)
¾ cup superfine sugar
3 eggs
2 teaspoons almond extract
1 teaspoon vanilla bean paste
1 cup jam—any flavor you like (I use raspberry)
sliced almonds, to decorate

1 Preheat the oven to 400°F and grease the baking pan.

2 Lightly flour a work surface. Roll out the dough into a rectangle large enough to cover the bottom of the baking pan, but don't worry if you don't have enough to go up the sides. It's just the bottom we need, and any rough edges will be covered by a layer of cake. Line the dough with foil, fill with pie weights or dried lentils or rice, and **blind bake** for 10 minutes. Remove the foil and weights, and bake for another 5 minutes to crisp it up. Remove from the oven and set aside. Reduce the oven to 350°F.

3 To make the cake layer, **cream** the butter and sugar together in a stand mixer or in a large bowl with an electric hand mixer. In a small bowl, whisk the eggs, almond extract, and vanilla paste together with a hand whisk, then gradually add to the creamed mixture, a little at a time, whisking constantly. Sift in the prepared flour and gently **fold** in.

4 Use a metal spatula or spoon to spread the jam onto the baked crust and then dollop the cake batter evenly on top, spreading it into the corners. Bake for 20 minutes, then scatter with the sliced almonds and bake for another 3 to 5 minutes.

5 Remove from the oven and slice into little bite-sized squares. Depending on the audience, I sometimes leave out the sliced almonds and opt for a simple water icing instead (made using equal quantities of powdered sugar and water mixed together until smooth). Some audiences call for both almonds AND icing.

Store in an airtight container at room temperature for up to 4 days.

Difficulty:

Jane's Legendary Carrot Cake

DO YOU KNOW JANE?

Jane is a family friend. Whenever she's around, so is her carrot cake. I have made a couple of edits to the method, forgive me Jane, but your flavors and ingredients have stayed the same. This is a good cake for teatime, and you can surprise your visitors with the unexpected coconut and pineapple. Within the carrot cake community, the question of whether or not to include raisins is a live and divisive issue. I don't like them, so I've opted not to.

KIT LIST
2 8-inch round cake pans
food processor (optional)
stand mixer or electric hand mixer
hand whisk
rubber spatula (optional)
Microplane (optional)

For the cake layers
unsalted butter, for greasing
¾ cup walnut halves
½ cup drained pineapple chunks from a can
1¼ cups grated carrots
1 cup desiccated coconut
2 cups all-purpose flour
1½ teaspoons baking soda
½ teaspoon salt
2 teaspoons ground cinnamon
1⅓ cups turbinado sugar
2 large eggs, beaten
¾ cup sunflower or corn oil
2 teaspoons vanilla extract

For the frosting
¾ stick unsalted butter, softened
⅓ cup cream cheese
2 cups powdered sugar, sifted, plus extra for dusting
1 teaspoon vanilla extract
1 teaspoon lemon juice
zest of 1 orange, some reserved to decorate

WAIT, THERE'S MORE... ➡

1 Preheat the oven to 400°F. Grease the cake pans and line the bottoms with parchment paper.

2 Chop the walnuts and pineapple chunks very finely or blitz in a food processor, then put into a bowl. Stir in the carrots and coconut. The mixture should look like a lumpy puree.

3 Sift together the flour, baking soda, salt, and cinnamon into the bowl of a stand mixer or a large bowl and add the sugar. Whisk until evenly combined. In a small bowl, beat the eggs and oil together with a hand whisk until combined, then stir in the vanilla extract. Gradually add the wet ingredients to the dry ingredients, a little at a time, whisking constantly with the mixer or an electric hand mixer. **Fold** in the carrot mixture until evenly distributed.

4 Divide the cake batter evenly between the pans and bake for 30 to 35 minutes, or until a skewer inserted into the middle comes out clean with no batter on it. Remove from the oven and the pans, then transfer to a wire rack to cool completely.

5 To make the frosting, beat the butter, cream cheese, and powdered sugar together until smooth. I find this easiest in a food processor (and it means you don't have to sift in the powdered sugar), but otherwise beat the butter and cream cheese together in your stand mixer or in a large bowl with the electric hand mixer, then sift in the powdered sugar and beat in. Add the vanilla extract, lemon juice, and orange zest and mix again.*

6 Peel the lining paper off of the cakes. Set one cake, bottom-side up, on a serving dish. Spread the top with frosting and stack the other cake on top of it. Dust the surface with powdered sugar and decorate with orange zest, to serve.

* It's important not to overwork the cream cheese, as it will become runny and ruin your frosting. If it's too late and the mixture is too liquidy to frost the cake, you'll need to sift in some more powdered sugar to thicken it. Be warned, this will make things very sweet, so balance out with some lemon juice if you can.

Store in an airtight container at room temperature for up to 3 days.

Difficulty:

Happle Cake

HONEY & APPLE, THE NEW POWER COUPLE

I'm not a massive fan of honey, but a colleague used to make a honey cake once a year and I couldn't get enough of it. So, I did a lot of research, because I'm a food geek and a history geek (an all-round geek really), and found lots of early examples of honey and mead cakes that served as good inspiration for my take on it. After much trial and error, and adding apple to balance out the sweetness, I ended up with this, which I'm very happle with.

KIT LIST
13-inch x 9-inch shallow baking pan
stand mixer or electric hand mixer
hand whisk
rubber spatula (optional)
small metal spatula

Ingredients
1⅓ sticks unsalted butter, softened
⅓ cup firmly packed soft light brown sugar
⅓ cup firmly packed soft dark brown sugar
2 eggs
½ cup crystallized honey
1⅔ cups all-purpose flour sifted with
    1½ teaspoons baking powder
½ teaspoon salt
1 teaspoon mixed spice (see page 194)
1 teaspoon ground ginger
1 cooking apple, peeled, cored, and cut
    into ½-inch cubes
3 tablespoons honey (optional)
yogurt, to serve

1 Preheat the oven to 350°F and line the baking pan with parchment paper.

2 Cream the butter and sugars together in a stand mixer or in a large bowl with an electric hand mixer for 5 minutes. In a separate bowl, whisk the eggs and crystallized honey together with a hand whisk until smooth, then gradually add to the creamed mixture, a little at a time, whisking constantly. Sift in the prepared flour, salt, and spices, add the apple, and then gently **fold** in to combine.

3 Transfer the batter to the lined pan, spread out evenly with a small metal spatula and bake for about 35 minutes until golden brown. Keep an eye on it in the latter stages of baking because the high sugar content means it will burn easily. Check it at 30 minutes and, if you need to, cover with foil for the final 5 minutes of baking.

4 Remove from the oven and top with the honey, if you like, letting it sink into the warm cake. Let cool completely in the pan. Serve in squares (or any shape that tickles you) with yogurt.

 Store in an airtight container at room temperature for up to 3 days.

Difficulty:

Banoffee Mess

BECAUSE, BELIEVE IT OR NOT, I DIDN'T GO TO ETON

One of my first jobs was working on weekends at a pub. I used to try and spend as much time in the kitchen as possible, especially when the chef was making desserts. This was the only thing he'd let me make, which should indicate just how easy it is. Things to bear in mind—this is incredibly sweet, so you need the nuts/ginger to give it a bit of earthy crunch. This CANNOT be made ahead of time because the meringue will melt, so make it, then eat it.

KIT LIST
stand mixer or electric hand mixer
rubber spatula (optional)

For the caramel sauce
1⅓ sticks unsalted butter
⅓ cup firmly packed soft light brown sugar
1 tablespoon water
3½ tablespoons evaporated milk

For the rest
1¼ cups heavy cream
3 ripe bananas, thinly sliced
4 ready-made vanilla meringues (or whip up a batch using the recipe for Eton Mess Gateaux on pages 54–5)
½ cup pecans, toasted and chopped (if you don't like nuts, try swapping this with chopped preserved ginger)

1 Start by making the caramel sauce because it needs to cool. You can even make this ahead of time and set it aside for a couple of hours so that this dessert can be whipped up, literally, in a matter of minutes.

2 Heat the butter, sugar, and measured water in a medium saucepan over medium heat and stir until the butter has melted. Bring to a gentle boil and continue boiling, stirring constantly, until the mixture has thickened and darkened, which normally takes about 8 minutes for me. Don't be afraid of it burning here. You need the sugar to melt (when you press a spatula against the side of the pan, you shouldn't feel any sugar crystals) and that takes a bit of time, and if you don't take it far enough, the sauce will be grainy. Once you are confident that the sugar has melted and the sauce is smooth, add the evaporated milk and stir vigorously while you bring the mixture to a boil, then remove from the heat and set aside to cool.

3 Whip the cream to **soft peaks*** in a stand mixer or in a large bowl with an electric hand mixer. Add the bananas and crumble in the meringues (save some for the topping). Be careful not to make them too small because they start to dissolve as soon as they hit the cream and you want a bit of crunch. Add the pecans or ginger (again save some for the topping) and stir to combine.

4 Pour in half of the caramel sauce and stir again. Serve in bowls or glasses, then top each portion with the remaining crumbled meringue, caramel, and chopped pecans or ginger. This makes 6 small portions. And you don't need much. Or it makes one large portion, which you can eat out of the bowl with a spoon.

Do not store; this is for eating right away.

✳ If you overwhip your cream and end up with **stiff peaks** (or, worse, lumps and weird milky water) then I'd like to direct you to the internet where somewhere, someone can show you how to use milk to save the day. That person is not me. I'd probably just keep going because by that point you've almost churned your own butter (which isn't useful for this recipe but waste not, want not).

Difficulty:

Irish Stout Cake

GOOD THINGS COME TO THOSE WHO WAIT

My cousin Jess was born on St. Patrick's Day, so we whip up an Irish stout cake to celebrate each year. She's not 18 yet, so it's technically still illegal for her to enjoy it, but that just means there's more for me. The Irish stout isn't an obvious taste but gives the cake an earthy undertone that results in a delicious, but not-too-sweet, chocolate cake. The frosting is just another opportunity to throw some Irish booze in there. This cake is beautifully light, which also makes it incredibly crumbly, so not one for carving.

KIT LIST
2 8-inch round cake pans
stand mixer or electric hand mixer
rubber spatula (optional)
food processor (optional)

For the cake layers
1¾ sticks unsalted butter, softened, plus
    extra for greasing
4½ ounces dark (semi-sweet) chocolate
    (54% cocoa solids minimum), broken
    into pieces
¾ cup firmly packed soft light brown sugar
¼ cup firmly packed soft dark brown sugar
2 eggs
1 cup Irish stout (I use Guinness)
2¼ cups all-purpose flour sifted with
    1 heaping tablespoon baking powder
½ cup unsweetened cocoa powder
2 tablespoons milk

For the frosting
½ cup cream cheese
1 stick unsalted butter, softened
2 cups powdered sugar
2 tablespoons Irish cream liqueur
    (I use Baileys)

 Best eaten on the day.

1 Preheat the oven to 375°F. Grease the cake pans and line the bases with parchment paper.

2 Melt the chocolate in a microwave-safe bowl in the microwave using the **heat, stir, repeat** method until smooth. Let cool.

3 **Cream** the butter and sugars together in a stand mixer or in a large bowl with an electric hand mixer for 5 minutes. Pour in the cooled melted chocolate and beat again. Add the eggs one at a time, beating well after each addition. Then gradually pour in the stout, whisking constantly.* Sift in the prepared flour and cocoa, then gently **fold** in to combine. Add the milk and fold in again.

4 Divide evenly between the prepared pans and bake for 25 minutes, or until a skewer inserted into the middle comes out clean. The tops will crack, but let the cakes cool completely in their pans and the cracks should close up as they cool.

5 To make the frosting, beat the cream cheese and butter together in your stand mixer or in a large bowl with the electric hand mixer, or in a food processor, until smooth. Be careful because it is very easy to overbeat the cream cheese and have it go irretrievably runny. Sift in the powdered sugar and then beat in. (I add the powdered sugar in 2 batches, beating after each addition, to prevent a powdered sugar cloud from coating all the surfaces in the kitchen.) Add the liqueur and beat again.

6 Remove the cooled cakes from their pans and peel off the paper. Turn both cakes bottom-side up and spread frosting on top of each. Stack one cake on top of the other to finish.

✳ Don't panic if your mixture looks odd and split;
it isn't the end of the world. To avoid this,
add a little of the flour from the next step
and beat again, which will smooth it out.

Difficulty: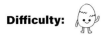

A Nice Vegan Dessert

NO, REALLY

This is a chocolate silken tofu mousse. I know. You weren't expecting it from me. Vegan baking is a dark art that I've not quite mastered (nor tried to). But when my vegan cousin from Germany started tucking into what I thought was a rich, creamy chocolate ganache that turned out to be made of tofu, my mind was blown. So if you're not vegan, don't be put off by the tofu. This is delicious as well as being quick, simple, and versatile. Eat it straight, with fruit, or slap it into a vegan pastry shell.

KIT LIST
food processor
ice-cream scoop (optional)

Ingredients
10½ ounces dairy-free dark chocolate
(if you like bitter chocolate, go as dark as you like, but I stick with 54% cocoa solids), broken into pieces
12 ounces silken tofu
2 tablespoons powdered sugar, sifted
1 tablespoon vanilla bean paste

To serve
chopped nuts
fresh berries or other fresh fruit

1 Melt the chocolate in a microwave-safe bowl in the microwave using the **heat, stir, repeat method** until smooth. Let cool.

2 Add the cooled melted chocolate to a food processor along with the tofu, powdered sugar, and vanilla paste, and blitz until smooth. You will need to give the mixture a stir occasionally to make sure there are no cheeky lumps of tofu left behind (you can totally get away without people knowing this is vegan, but these lumps will give it away).

3 Transfer to a bowl, cover with plastic wrap, and refrigerate until ready to serve. I serve using an ice-cream scoop to make balls and plate up with chopped nuts, raspberries, and strawberries.

 Store in the fridge for up to 4 days.

Difficulty:

Cheese Dream

PROUDLY SPONSORED BY BUTTER

This is a fried cheese sandwich. I'm not ashamed to put it in the book because it's one of the few things that makes me sentimental. Sunday morning memories with mother and all that stuff. My great-grandmother used bacon fat instead of butter, but I'm not sure many of us have that lying around these days. Works really well with the Chili & Garlic Loaf on page 114, but experiment with whatever bread you like.

KIT LIST
large cookie cutter, at least 2 inches

Ingredients
butter, softened, for spreading, plus a
   walnut-sized lump for frying
4 slices of brown bread
3½ ounces sharp cheddar cheese, sliced
cracked black pepper

1 Butter both sides of all 4 slices of bread. Put the cheese on 2 slices and season with cracked black pepper. Top with the remaining slices of bread to make 2 sandwiches.

2 Using a large cookie cutter, stamp out 2 circles from each sandwich. Heat a large skillet to medium heat and add the walnut-sized lump of butter. Reduce to low heat, add the sandwich circles, and fry for 3 to 4 minutes on each side.*

✳ Because of the high fat content, this will brown very quickly, so peep underneath occasionally and flip sooner if it looks like it is starting to burn.

 These aren't for storing. They're for eating straightaway.

Difficulty:

Back & Crack Scotch Eggs

MARGINALLY LESS PAINFUL THAN A WAX

I'm really pleased with this title, although I am expecting to open a final copy of the book to see that it's been removed by my editors. To explain... back is a reference to back bacon, aka pork. And crack is a reference to the egg. A collaboration with my Uncle Steve, this recipe uses quail eggs because it takes less meat to cover them, meaning they take less time to cook, and you're more likely to hang on to a deliciously oozy yolk. You'll need to keep your wits about you as deep-frying is involved. These were a school sports day staple, which might explain why I never won any races.

KIT LIST
slotted spoon
thermometer

Ingredients
splash of white wine vinegar
ice cubes
8 quail eggs, plus spares—you WILL
    lose at least one when peeling
    off the shells
6 of your favorite pork sausages—
    breakfast sausage, bratwurst, Italian,
    chorizo, wild boar, or whatever you like
1 tablespoon dried sage, or more if the
    sausages are not already flavored
1 tablespoon onion granules
1 teaspoon cracked black pepper
¼ teaspoon salt
1 egg, beaten
2½ cups panko breadcrumbs
¾ cup all-purpose flour
oil, for deep-frying

1 Bring a saucepan of water to a boil with a splash of white wine vinegar (this softens the egg shell and makes them easier to remove—shout out to Chef Tom Brown for that tip). Fill a bowl with cold water and add some ice. When the water is boiling, lower in the quail eggs and boil for 2 minutes*. Remove from the water with a slotted spoon and add the eggs to the bowl of iced water. Once cold, remove and shell the eggs, then set aside.

2 Split the sausages with a knife and remove the meat from the skin. Discard the skin and put the meat into a large bowl. Add the sage, onion granules, black pepper, and salt and mix together until well combined. Don't be afraid to use your hands on this one. However, don't go licking your fingers, and be sure to remember to wash your hands after you've been handling the raw meat. Cover the bowl with plastic wrap and let the seasoned sausagemeat chill in the fridge for about 10 minutes.

> ✳If you want to try and achieve a soft-boiled egg, boil your eggs for 1 minute, turn off the heat, and let them sit in the water for 30 seconds, then plunge into iced water. I am warning you though, this makes the eggs incredibly delicate and it's even harder to peel off the shells. I lost 3 doing this, and a cooked egg is better than no egg at all. In my opinion.

3 You are now going to set up a little production line. Put your beaten egg, breadcrumbs, and flour into 3 separate bowls. Take a ping-pong-ball-sized amount of sausagemeat, flatten it in your palm, and then set an egg in the middle. Gently (very gently, as these eggs are delicate) start to seal the sausagemeat around the egg, pinching it closed. Roll back into a ball shape in your hand, then roll in the flour bowl, roll in the beaten egg bowl, roll in the breadcrumb bowl, and voilà—your first Scotch egg is ready for frying. Repeat with the remaining sausagemeat and eggs.

4 Half-fill a deep saucepan with oil for deep-frying and heat to 350°F. Line a plate with paper towels. I find it difficult to maintain the oil temperature without either burning the house down or making everything soggy, so I heat it to reach the temperature, turn it down to stop it from going over 350°F, then bring it back up to temperature before frying. When the oil is ready, lower in the first 2 Scotch eggs using a slotted spoon and time for 6 minutes.** Very carefully roll the eggs while they are frying to ensure even cooking. Remove from the oil and place on the lined plate to drain. Repeat with the remaining Scotch eggs. Let cool for a good 5 minutes before attempting to eat them.

✱✱ If the oil isn't hot enough, the Scotch eggs will immediately become soggy and a write-off. So it's important that before you lower in your next 2, you test that the oil is at a high enough temperature. To do this, drop in a breadcrumb and make sure it fizzes on the surface.

CHECK OUT THE PHOTO → →

 Store in the fridge for up to 2 days.

Difficulty:

Mrs. B's Onion Biscuits

THEY'VE GOT A FACE FOR RADIO

These are inspired by recipes I inherited from both my grandmothers. In the same way real estate agents say "viewing recommended" when they want you to look at a flat that's got terrible pictures but is apparently breathtaking in real life, these come with a "tasting recommended" qualifier. Because they look ugly. But they taste really good. And they're a much better use of your time than traipsing round overpriced studio flats that overlook junk stores (trust me).

KIT LIST
cookie sheet
metal spatula (optional)
sharp 2½-inch cookie cutter (optional)

Ingredients
1 stick unsalted butter
2 cups grated sharp cheddar cheese
1⅔ cups dried or crispy onions
1 cup all-purpose flour, plus extra for dusting
pinch of cayenne pepper
chutney, to serve (optional)

1 Melt the butter In a large saucepan, remove from the heat, and add the cheddar. Stir well so that the cheese starts to melt. Transfer to a large bowl, stir in the onions, flour, and cayenne and mix until well combined.

2 Generously flour a work surface, then turn the mixture out onto it and bring together with your hands to form a dough. Roll into a long sausage 2½ inches in diameter (you might find it easier to do this with half the dough at a time), seal in plastic wrap, and let chill in the fridge for 45 minutes.

3 Preheat the oven to 410°F and line a cookie sheet with parchment paper. Slice the dough into thin rounds (about ⅛ inch thick if possible) and place on the lined cookie sheet. Using a metal spatula might be helpful here, as they are very delicate.* And you will need to pat them back into circles with your fingers once on the cookie sheet. Bake for 10 to 12 minutes, or until golden brown.

4 Transfer to a wire rack and let cool, then try and eat fewer than 3 at a time.

> ✳ If the dough is too crumbly to cut the sausage into rounds, roll it out to a thickness of about ⅛ inch, flouring the top of the dough if it's sticking, and use the SHARP cookie cutter (it will need to get through the onion bits) to stamp out circles. Carefully transfer these to the lined cookie sheet, again patting the biscuits back into circles if you need to.

 Store in an airtight container at room temperature for up to 3 days.

Index

ACKNOWLEDGMENTS

With thanks to:

Sasa, Steve, Leo, and Jess; Nana & Papa; my mother; Emily Roberts; Hampstead Theatre; Dan Marks; Elly James and Heather Holden-Brown; my dad & Tina; and all of the "Pass It On, Please" contributors.

And a special thanks to my recipe testers:

Jack, Jon, Dub, Lucie, Abe, Elsie, Becky, Sue, Joe, Daisy, Lizzie, Jo, Grace, Alice, Scott, Edith, Ursula, Catriona, Assunta, Sam, Hannah, Ilaria, Katharine, "Laura off of *Bake Off*," and, last but by no means least, Amelia, without whom this book would never have been delivered on time.